OPPOSING
VIEWPOINTS®
SERIES

The US Census

Other Books of Related Interest:

Opposing Viewpoints Series

Illegal Immigration

Interracial America

Population

The US Latino Community

Urban America

Welfare

At Issue Series

Is Socialism Harmful?

Current Controversies Series

Illegal Immigration

Politics and the Media

U.S. Government Corruption

Global Viewpoints Series

Democracy

"Congress shall make
no law . . . abridging
the freedom of speech,
or of the press."

First Amendment to the US Constitution

The basic foundation of our democracy is the First Amendment guarantee of freedom of expression. The Opposing Viewpoints series is dedicated to the concept of this basic freedom and the idea that it is more important to practice it than to enshrine it.

OPPOSING
VIEWPOINTS®
SERIES

I The US Census

David Haugen, Susan Musser, and Ross M. Berger,
Book Editors

GREENHAVEN PRESS
A part of Gale, Cengage Learning

GALE
CENGAGE Learning·

Detroit • New York • San Francisco • New Haven, Conn • Waterville, Maine • London

Elizabeth Des Chenes, *Managing Editor*

© 2012 Greenhaven Press, a part of Gale, Cengage Learning.

Gale and Greenhaven Press are registered trademarks used herein under license.

For more information, contact:
Greenhaven Press
27500 Drake Rd.
Farmington Hills, MI 48331-3535
Or you can visit our Internet site at gale.cengage.com

For product information and technology assistance, contact us at

Gale Customer Support, 1-800-877-4253
For permission to use material from this text or product, submit all requests online at www.cengage.com/permissions

Further permissions questions can be emailed to permissionrequest@cengage.com

Articles in Greenhaven Press anthologies are often edited for length to meet page require-ments. In addition, original titles of these works are changed to clearly present the main thesis and to explicitly indicate the author's opinion. Every effort is made to ensure that Greenhaven Press accurately reflects the original intent of the authors. Every effort has been made to trace the owners of copyrighted material.

Cover Image copyright © Gemenacom/Shutterstock.com.

LIBRARY OF CONGRESS CATALOGING-IN-PUBLICATION DATA

The US census / David Haugen, Susan Musser, and Ross M. Berger, book editors.
    p. cm. -- (Opposing viewpoints)
    Includes bibliographical references and index.
    ISBN 978-0-7377-5765-1 (hardcover) -- ISBN 978-0-7377-5766-8 (pbk.)
    1. United States. Bureau of the Census. 2. United States--Census--Evaluation. I.
Haugen, David M., 1969- II. Musser, Susan. III. Berger, Ross M.
    HA37.U55U7 2012
    352.7'50973--dc23
                                                              2011038303

Printed in the United States of America
1 2 3 4 5 6 7 16 15 14 13 12

Contents

Chapter 3: How Should the US Census Be Reformed?

Why Consider
Opposing Viewpoints?

> "The only way in which a human being can make some approach to knowing the whole of a subject is by hearing what can be said about it by persons of every variety of opinion and studying all modes in which it can be looked at by every character of mind. No wise man ever acquired his wisdom in any mode but this."
>
> John Stuart Mill

In our media-intensive culture it is not difficult to find differing opinions. Thousands of newspapers and magazines and dozens of radio and television talk shows resound with differing points of view. The difficulty lies in deciding which opinion to agree with and which "experts" seem the most credible. The more inundated we become with differing opinions and claims, the more essential it is to hone critical reading and thinking skills to evaluate these ideas. Opposing Viewpoints books address this problem directly by presenting stimulating debates that can be used to enhance and teach these skills. The varied opinions contained in each book examine many different aspects of a single issue. While examining these conveniently edited opposing views, readers can develop critical thinking skills such as the ability to compare and contrast authors' credibility, facts, argumentation styles, use of persuasive techniques, and other stylistic tools. In short, the Opposing Viewpoints Series is an ideal way to attain the higher-level thinking and reading skills so essential in a culture of diverse and contradictory opinions.

In addition to providing a tool for critical thinking, Opposing Viewpoints books challenge readers to question their own strongly held opinions and assumptions. Most people form their opinions on the basis of upbringing, peer pressure, and personal, cultural, or professional bias. By reading carefully balanced opposing views, readers must directly confront new ideas as well as the opinions of those with whom they disagree. This is not to argue simplistically that everyone who reads opposing views will—or should—change his or her opinion. Instead, the series enhances readers' understanding of their own views by encouraging confrontation with opposing ideas. Careful examination of others' views can lead to the readers' understanding of the logical inconsistencies in their own opinions, perspective on why they hold an opinion, and the consideration of the possibility that their opinion requires further evaluation.

Evaluating Other Opinions

To ensure that this type of examination occurs, Opposing Viewpoints books present all types of opinions. Prominent spokespeople on different sides of each issue as well as well-known professionals from many disciplines challenge the reader. An additional goal of the series is to provide a forum for other, less known, or even unpopular viewpoints. The opinion of an ordinary person who has had to make the decision to cut off life support from a terminally ill relative, for example, may be just as valuable and provide just as much insight as a medical ethicist's professional opinion. The editors have two additional purposes in including these less known views. One, the editors encourage readers to respect others' opinions—even when not enhanced by professional credibility. It is only by reading or listening to and objectively evaluating others' ideas that one can determine whether they are worthy of consideration. Two, the inclusion of such viewpoints encourages the important critical thinking skill of objectively evaluating an author's credentials and bias. This evaluation will illuminate an author's reasons for taking a particular stance on an issue and will aid in readers' evaluation of the author's ideas.

It is our hope that these books will give readers a deeper understanding of the issues debated and an appreciation of the complexity of even seemingly simple issues when good and honest people disagree. This awareness is particularly important in a democratic society such as ours in which people enter into public debate to determine the common good. Those with whom one disagrees should not be regarded as enemies but rather as people whose views deserve careful examination and may shed light on one's own.

Thomas Jefferson once said that "difference of opinion leads to inquiry, and inquiry to truth." Jefferson, a broadly educated man, argued that "if a nation expects to be ignorant and free . . . it expects what never was and never will be." As individuals and as a nation, it is imperative that we consider the opinions of others and examine them with skill and discernment. The Opposing Viewpoints series is intended to help readers achieve this goal.

David L. Bender and Bruno Leone,
Founders

Introduction

"While taking the census sounds simple and straightforward, it is anything but. The scope and complexity of the census has steadily increased. It is the largest peacetime mobilization in the United States."

—Former US secretary of commerce Carlos M. Gutierrez, statement before the United States House Appropriations Subcommittee on Commerce, Justice, Science, and Related Agencies, April 3, 2008

"I am proud of the American people for understanding the importance of the census to their communities and participating at much greater numbers than anyone expected."

—Current US secretary of commerce Gary Locke, remarks at 2010 Census Operational Press Briefing, August 10, 2010

Excitement may not necessarily be the first word most people associate when they think of the US census. Unlike health care or national defense, assessing the nation's population seems to lack controversy, on the surface, perhaps because the act itself might seem pedestrian. However, its critics do not shy away from making a heated debate of what was originally conceived of as a simple head count of the nation's population.

According to Article I, Section II of the US Constitution, the government is required by law to undertake a census every ten years to enumerate the number of its citizens. The results dictate how many districts and, accordingly, how many individuals will serve in the House of Representatives from each state. These figures also determine how many electoral votes each state carries during the presidential election. Therefore, the results of the US census are crucial in deciding the future of the nation's leadership.

The enumeration of the American people every ten years is known as a "decennial" population count. According to the website of the US Census Bureau, when the first census was taken on August 2, 1790, the following information was sought from each household: "the name of the head of the family and the number of persons in each household" and specifically how many of those in the household qualified as "free White males of 16 years and upward ... free White males under 16 years, free White females, all other free persons (by sex and color), and slaves." Ignoring any contentions over the separation of free men and slaves, those questions not only determined how many people lived in each household but also who was eligible to serve in the military.

By 1820, the census began including questions concerning the country's expanding economy and, thus, sought information about an individual's involvement in agriculture, commerce, or manufacturing. Thirty years later, the census took into consideration "social statistics" by covering such topics as a participant's tax status and level of schooling. It also asked each individual if he or she had committed any crimes or was living in poverty. Later in the century, the census started to include questions of country origin and language proficiency, reflecting the country's new wave of immigration.

By 2010, the US census asked no more than ten questions and sought, in part, the following information: the individual's name, date of birth, gender, relation to the head of the household, the type of home the person lives in, and his or her racial background. Other data is now gathered continuously between decades by smaller branches within the federal government. Such branches include the American Community Survey, an annual survey conducted by the US Census Bureau, and the Current Population Survey, a monthly survey conducted by the Bureau of Labor Statistics that gathers information on consumer spending and employment status.

The decennial US census and the American Community Survey are crucial in determining the amount of federal and state funding a community may receive for infrastructure, education, public health, transportation, and other neighborhood needs. In 2010, the data determined where $400 billion in federal and state subsidies would be distributed. Some critics fear that such a high expenditure is vulnerable to political manipulation. Larry J. Sabato, director of the Center for Politics at the University of Virginia, believes that "the last thing the census needs is for any hard-bitten partisan ... to manipulate these critical numbers. Many federal funding formulas depend on them, as well as the whole fabric of federal and state representation. Partisans have a natural impulse to tilt the playing field in their favor, and this has to be resisted."

Fears of misappropriation of funds based on census data may not be unfounded. The 2008 renovation of the Blackstone Hotel in Chicago is often touted as a case in point. Manipulation of poverty statistics from the 2000 census allowed insurance firm Prudential Financial Inc. to gain a $15.6 million tax credit from the Department of the Treasury. Under a program called New Markets Tax Credit, Prudential used that money to help fund the two-year, $116 million renovation of this high-end hotel, miles away from (though, in the same district as) impoverished neighborhoods in dire need of such a subsidy. This is just one example of many, suggest Bloomberg news editors Jonathan Neumann and Gail Roche, in which financial institutions have taken advantage of federal funding. In their February 8, 2009, report, the editors remark, "Money spent on high-end development could have been used to build more than 1,000 job-training centers, medical clinics and schools."

Excluding claims of misappropriation, though, the worth of accurate census reporting has made itself clear in regard to underrepresented or underprivileged groups. Melissa Olson, writing for the monthly Native American publication *The Circle* on March 11, 2010, reports that the 2000 census yielded an undercounted Native American demographic in the Minneapolis and St. Paul areas of Minnesota. This resulted in the reduction of necessary services such as the Workforce Investment Act, which provides critical job training and retention services. Increased participation is more critical for 2010, as Olson writes, "Due to recent changes in the U.S. economy, organizations and non-profits addressing Native issues find they are increasingly strapped for funds."

There have been other examples in which the US census worked against those of minority status. According to law, the US Census Bureau protects an individual's microdata—which includes a person's race and ethnicity—from collection by other governmental agencies, not-for-profit organizations, and private entities. However, during the height of World War II, the Second War Powers Act of 1942 suspended such protective measures and made it possible for the Secret Service to gain access to census microdata identifying Japanese Americans. In a March 30, 2007, article for *Scientific American*, JR Minkel holds that this appropriation of census data was part of a government effort to "assist in the roundup of Japanese-Americans for imprisonment in internment camps in California and six other states during the war." By 1952, however, then census director Roy V. Peel established the "72-year Rule," which prevents the public (Secret Service included) from accessing an individual's personal information from a decennial census until seventy-two years after the fact, when such data will be released to the public by the National Archives and Records Administration.

By 2004, the Department of Homeland Security continued where the Secret Service left off in the 1940s; however, this time the focus was on Arab Americans. According to Haya El Nasser of *USA Today*, "The Census turned over information it had collected about Arab-Americans by ZIP code but not by name." Although this data sharing was within the confines of the law, the outcry by the Arab American population and civil rights groups compelled the US Census Bureau to adopt stricter standards before releasing data to other government agencies.

In *Opposing Viewpoints: The US Census*, numerous writers and experts tackle the many controversies surrounding the census and its fundamental purposes. Moreover, authorities cited herein offer new measures upon which the US census may be improved in administering and gathering its data. In chapters titled Is the US Census Useful?, Does the US Census Accurately Represent the Country's Population?, and How Should the US Census Be Reformed?, these experts recognize the challenges that can arise from partisan boycotts, controversial statistical sampling methods, undocumented immigrant enumeration racial categorization, and other subjects. They also provide thought-provoking questions supported by rigorous research, highlighting how the system of head counting the American populace is still crucial in identifying the needs of the nation's diverse—and sometimes underserved—communities.

Since the census is a permanent and necessary instrument to assist in the governance of the nation, this anthology suggests that one of the duties of the government and the Census Bureau is figuring out how best to count the country's ever-changing population without violating the privacy of the citizenry. So, too, must the census concern itself with a thorough and fair enumeration of the people, striving to document hard-to-count segments of society and thus ensuring that everyone in America receives the benefits of representation.

CHAPTER 1

Is the US Census Useful?

Chapter Preface

The US census was initially mandated by the Constitution to count citizens to determine the apportioning of seats in the House of Representatives. Although the population count now impacts other aspects of civic significance, including the distribution of federal funds, a great deal of the controversy spawned by the census still centers on the issue of representation. Since the early formation of the United States, the census has been most prominently tied to political opportunism through the process of gerrymandering.

Gerrymandering is the act of political leveraging and manipulation to maintain or create electoral districts that favor a specific political party. Those who seek this advantage commonly use census data—particularly a district's gender, racial, and ethnic breakdowns—to help their party determine voter demographic strengths and thereby redistrict territories based upon those likely to vote for desired candidates. Census data may indicate a strong partiality for a specific party—a boon for politicians of that stripe. However, census data might also indicate that too many people have fled a district to warrant one or more representatives, a potential loss for that party. In cases of population loss—or population gain—the states may have to redistrict regions to account for the change, and such redrawing of electoral boundaries may add or subtract from the number of state representatives in the House.

Even though gerrymandering has been a part of the political landscape for centuries, scholars still debate whether the practice is constitutional. In the Supreme Court case *League of United Latin American Citizens v. Perry* (2006), the majority ruled that the state of Texas (or any state, for that matter) may redistrict however it likes as long as it happens every ten years; yet, the Supreme Court struck down (in that same case) the redistricting of certain Latino-heavy districts in Texas because they violated federal law, particularly the Voting Rights Act. Justice Anthony Kennedy argued that the redrawn district in question was reconstructed in such a way as to stymie the opportunity for Latino voters as a group to elect a candidate of their choice by splitting the district in two.

Although the issue of race was significant in the Texas case, the incident was not deemed racial gerrymandering, which is a direct violation of the Equal Protection Clause of the Fourteenth Amendment. To qualify for that illegal practice, a whole district would have to have been created based solely on race, as stated in another Supreme Court case, *Shaw v. Reno* (1993). The difference between these two cases is the state's creation of a new, unfair benefit (racially drawn districts in *Shaw*) vs. the state's act to remove an established benefit unfairly (splitting up a minority-heavy district in *League of United Latin American Citizens v. Perry*).

Despite its questionable constitutionality, racial gerrymandering has its advocates. Senator Scott Brown of Massachusetts wants his home state to create an additional district (a majority-minority district where the majority of voters are nonwhites) by the 2012 election. When Brown announced, "I want to add my vote to theirs," he was pushing for an additional minority voice in Congress that can help address the needs of those underserved by government. It is suggested that additional representation can lead to funding, altered polices, and enhanced awareness on issues affecting minority communities.

Critics like political advisor Thomas Young would not endorse such redistricting. In his article for Mississippi's *Meridian Star* titled "Racial Gerrymandering: Good or Bad?," Young believes that heavily gerrymandered districts based on race will never benefit minorities elected to a state or congressional office because "they are unlikely to have wide appeal necessary to win stateside offices." He also believes a candidate has a better chance of excelling if he or she comes from a diverse district because that candidate has learned to develop a message that appeals to people of different backgrounds as opposed to those of the same. Then, candidates will have to "base their appeal upon character and what they seek to accomplish in office."

Disputes over the practice of gerrymandering will continue to haunt the census, forcing Americans to question whether the age-old head count is serving the purpose for which it was originally intended. The authors in the following chapter engage with other questions, most of which still connect to the overriding issue of representation, concerning the utility of the census.

| *"Who wants to hand out $400+ billion a year based on unacceptably inaccurate data?"*

The Census Provides Essential Information to the Government

Terri Ann Lowenthal

A former staff director of the census oversight subcommittee in the US House of Representatives, Terri Ann Lowenthal serves as a consultant to many civic programs, including the Census Project, a nonpartisan organization working to ensure a fair and accurate census. In the viewpoint that follows, Lowenthal claims that the American Community Survey (ACS)—the "long form" census document mailed to three million US citizens each year—provides necessary statistical data that the government uses to fund various projects, from drug treatment programs to public transit. Lowenthal maintains that arguments against the survey—based on the assumption that the information-gathering process is intrusive—are wrongheaded and a glaring case of partisan politics.

As you read, consider the following questions:

1. According to Lowenthal, what are some of the issues that Congress and the states address using census data?

2. As Lowenthal asserts, what political faction wants to eliminate the ACS because it supposedly is "an invasion of privacy"?

3. What is the aim of the Poe bill (H.R. 3131), as the author explains?

L ast week [in August 2010] I patiently explained how the Census Bureau's American Community Survey (ACS) asks *nosy sounding* questions in order to produce a bank of knowledge that can help improve our quality of life and the future for our children. Those questions are merely building blocks to measure the prevalence of overcrowded and unaffordable housing; areas of heavy traffic during prime commuting hours; neighborhoods with low vehicle ownership that need more public transit; the location of people with health challenges who might require additional services or extra attention by disaster response planners—data that policy makers can use to make wise (hopefully . . . you can lead a horse to water but you can't make him drink) decisions.

Complaints Against the Census

But not everyone thinks objective, reliable information is a useful tool for decision makers. As the *New York Times* reported the day after my blog post, the Republican National Committee (RNC) has adopted a resolution calling for outright elimination of the ACS or, failing that draconian step, voluntary response to the survey (it is currently mandatory, under the same law that requires response to the decennial census). Mindlessly calling the ACS an "invasion of privacy," the resolution accuses the survey of "demand[ing] detailed personal information that the government has no business

The American Community Survey (ACS) Provides Information on a Yearly Basis

Income and Benefits (ACS data for Silver Spring CDP, Maryland, 2006)

Income and benefits - ACS	Income	+/- Margin of error
Total households	29,720	1,933
Less than $10K	1,383	551
$10K to $14,999	992	532
$15K to $24,999	2,019	700
$25K to $34,999	3,559	1,090
$35K to $49,999	3,591	941
$50K to $74,999	6,515	1,271
$75K to $99,999	3,743	909
$100K to $149,999	3,879	994
$150K to $199,999	1,883	613
$200K or more	2,156	656
Median household income (dollars)	61,649	6,695
Mean household income (dollars)	82,006	6,519

TAKEN FROM: Chris Williamson, "Counting Down to 2010: Not Your Mother's Census," *Planning*, November 2008.

seeking, knowing, or compiling" (take that, Census Bureau!) and goes on to offer a laundry list of the supposedly offending queries.

Coincidentally, Canada just decided to make its version of the census long form voluntary. The nation's chief statistician promptly resigned in protest. On this side of the border, the Republican Party has now taken to calling the nation's premier statistical agency a "scam artist" for gathering data that members of Congress from both parties have required it to collect *by law*. It has questioned the Census Bureau's commitment to protecting the confidentiality of all personal information and falsely accused the agency of sharing personal information with other government agencies or selling it (say what?). It has accused a scientific agency of "overreaching" and of "intimidating" the public to participate in what is, *by law*, a mandatory survey. Hey, maybe we too can drive top scientific minds from public service. Way to go, RNC!

(Inexplicably, the resolution digresses with a reference to the Fourth Amendment's protection against "unreasonable searches and seizures," which has to do with the issuance of warrants, before resuming its rant against "very specific questions" on the ACS. Is the RNC suggesting that the Census Bureau seek a judicial warrant before mailing out a survey? Excuse me, but I think I am getting a headache. . . .)

But this is no laughing matter. I think the Republican National Committee has lost its mind. The resolution clearly was orchestrated by virulent limited-government, anti-knowledge party members, and yet party leaders stepped aside and allowed this thoughtless tirade to become an official party position. In turning a blind eye, they have thrown any pretense of having a rational debate about why and how we collect data to the winds.

Census Data Is Used to Direct Government Funding

Now, let's pause for a moment to consider the consequences of the RNC's proposal. As the Brookings Institution [a nonprofit, public policy organization] reported this summer, $416 billion in fiscal year 2008 federal program funds were allocated to states and localities using data from the American Community Survey. Almost $2.9 billion of that total went to Harris County, Texas, represented in part by Rep. Ted Poe (R-TX), sponsor of a bill (H.R. 3131)—along with Rep. Michele "Just the Number of People in My Household" Bachmann (R-MN)—to make response to all but four basic questions on the ACS voluntary. The RNC resolution, which endorses the Poe bill, doesn't tell us how we might distribute funds for housing for persons with disabilities and the elderly, compensatory education grants (Title I) to school districts, highway planning and construction, assistance with home fuel costs to low-income households, and substance abuse prevention and treatment programs, without data from the ACS.

Did I mention that Rep. Poe, a former judge, founded the Congressional Victims' Rights Caucus? The Justice Department allocated $302 million in Crime Victim Assistance grants in 2008 using ACS data. Did I mention that the congressman, also a former prosecutor, cares deeply about preventing and addressing crime, noting as a cosponsor of National Criminal Justice Month in 2008 that government spends billions of dollars on the criminal justice system? "The cost of crime is not cheap," Rep. Poe said in a statement, ". . . the price is worth it to ensure order, safety, and appropriate punishment for those who fail to follow the law." The state of Texas received $32 million in 2008 to help keep communities safe, based on ACS data alone (there are millions of dollars more allocated using decennial census data and annual population estimates, which themselves rely on the ACS for components of international migration).

And (please bear with me here) let's not forget that in 2003, at Congress' direction, the Census Bureau tested the possibility of making response to the ACS voluntary. In a nutshell, the test revealed that cooperation by mail and telephone fell substantially when response was voluntary, diminishing reliability of the statistics and increasing the survey's cost by about a third. (Show of hands: Who wants to hand out $400+ billion a year based on unacceptably inaccurate data?)

Hoping Some Republicans Will Support the Census

The RNC will distribute its resolution to Republican office holders and party officials at all levels of government. Will any Republican members of Congress have the courage to disagree publicly with this party diatribe? Will any of them have the

"Census Bureau: Out for the Count," cartoon by Chris Patterson, www.CartoonStock .com. Copyright © by Chris Patterson. Reproduction rights obtainable from www.Car toonStock.com.

decency to let the party faithful know that they share respon-sibility for the survey's breadth? Will any of them defend the Census Bureau against the baseless charges of violating confi-dentiality and using intimidation and unethical tactics in the conduct of its scientific work?

Rep. Patrick McHenry (R-NC), ranking Republican on the Census Bureau's oversight subcommittee? Sen. Susan Collins (R-ME) and Sen. John McCain (R-AZ) of the agency's over-sight committee in the Senate? Rep. Charles Dent (R-PA) and Sen. Tom Coburn (R-OK), cosponsors of a bipartisan bill to give the Census Bureau *more* autonomy to carry out its work free from political interference under an administration of ei-ther party? We are waiting.

And I am waiting for [former governor of Alaska and former 2008 candidate for vice president on the Republican ticket] Sarah Palin's tweet on this whole ACS controversy. "Don't need gov't asking nosy questions. Mama Grizzlies just *no* [sic] how many people are poor and need a job. Send federal $$$ to Alaska, quick!"

"*Everywhere we look these days, we are either being watched, taxed or some bureaucrat is placing another bit of information in our government files. Now with the American Community Survey, the federal bureaucracy is thrusting its expansive tentacles toward us in an attempt to invade every aspect of our lives.*"

The Census Survey Asks Intrusive, Unnecessary Questions

John W. Whitehead

In the following viewpoint, John W. Whitehead claims the American Community Survey (ACS)—a yearly and more detailed census document sent to millions of Americans—is intrusive and unconstitutional. According to Whitehead, the survey asks many personal questions that concern everything from income to mental health, giving the government a large quantity of data that could possibly be used against those who take the survey. Whitehead claims the purpose of the traditional census—which is ad-

ministered every ten years—is solely to apportion congressional representation. Anything beyond that is, in his view, a sign of greater government control over citizens' lives. Whitehead is an attorney and the author of such works as An American Dream *and* The Second American Revolution.

As you read, consider the following questions:

1. How many pages long is the American Community Survey (ACS), as Whitehead reveals?

2. According to Whitehead, since the ACS is compulsory, what is the potential fine for each question a recipient does not answer?

3. In what way does Whitehead compare the ACS to George Orwell's novel *Nineteen Eighty-Four?*

Over the past several years, I have been barraged with e-mails from Americans expressing their dismay over the American Community Survey, the latest census form to hit randomly selected households on a continuous basis. Unlike the traditional census, which collects data every ten years and is now under way, the American Community Survey is taken every year at a cost of hundreds of millions of dollars. And at 28 pages (with an additional 16-page instruction packet), it contains some of the most detailed and intrusive questions ever put forth in a census questionnaire. These concern matters that the government simply has no business knowing, including a person's job, income, physical and emotional health, family status, place of residence and intimate personal and private habits.

A Compulsory Survey of Private Lives

As one frustrated survey recipient, Beth, shared with me:

> When we first read through the American Community Survey, we thought it was an ID theft scam. I showed it to a

lawyer friend of mine. She had never heard of the survey and warned it could be a scam. She said if she'd received this, she would call her congressman and senator to find out if scams such as this were happening to warn others. So I called Washington, DC. They in turn told me to call our senator's office in my state—which I did. I was referred to the Justice Department, who then referred me to my county representative. When I called my county representative, my call was shifted to a Census Bureau employee placed in their offices to field questions about the survey. The Census Bureau representative told me the survey was not a scam. She could not tell me whether or not to fill it out, but said if we chose not to, there could be hefty fines and jail time associated with not doing so. She was no help at all and was evasive in answering my questions.

As Beth found out, the survey is not voluntary. Answering the questions is not a polite request from the Census Bureau. You are legally obligated to answer. If you refuse, the fines are staggering. For every question not answered, there is a $100 fine. And for every intentionally false response to a question, the fine is $500. Therefore, if a person representing a two-person household refused to fill out any questions or simply answered nonsensically, the total fines could range from upwards of $10,000 and $50,000 for noncompliance.

While the penalties for not answering are outrageous, the questions, as Rep. Ron Paul (R-Texas) has said, are "both ludicrous and insulting." For example, the survey asks how many persons live in your home, along with their names and detailed information about them such as their relationship to you, marital status, race and their physical, mental and emotional problems, etc. The survey also asks how many bedrooms and bathrooms you have in your house, along with the kind of fuel used to heat your home, the cost of electricity, what type of mortgage you have, the amount of your monthly mortgage payments, property taxes and so on. This questionnaire also requires you to detail how many days you were sick last year, how many automobiles you own, whether you have trouble getting up the stairs and, amazingly, what time you leave for work every morning and how long it takes you to get there. When faced with the prospect that government agents could covertly enter your home and rifle through your personal belongings, do you really want the government knowing exactly when you're away from home?

Spying on Friends and Family

As if the survey's asinine questions and highly detailed inquiries into your financial affairs weren't bad enough, you're also expected to violate the privacy of others by supplying the names and addresses of your friends, relatives and employer. And the questionnaire stipulates that you provide such information on the people in your home as their educational levels, how many years of schooling they completed, what languages they speak and when they last worked at a job, among other things.

Americans being ordered by the government to inform and spy on your family and friends? It's not too far off from the scenario George Orwell envisioned in his futuristic novel *Nineteen Eighty-Four*. "The family," writes Orwell, "had become in effect an extension of the Thought Police. It was a device by means of which everyone could be surrounded night and day by informers who knew him intimately."

Another Aspect of the Surveillance State

Granted, some of the questions in the American Community Survey may appear fairly routine. However, the danger rests in not knowing exactly how the government plans to use this vast amount of highly personal information. For instance, if the financial information you provide on the survey does not jive with your tax returns, whether such a discrepancy was intentional or not, could you be flagged for an IRS [Internal Revenue Service] audit? Given the increasing amount of collusion taking place between government agencies in recent years, I wouldn't rule it out.

The Census Is Another Surveillance Tool

Can freedom flourish while government amasses knowledge about us, even if restricted to an "Enumeration" alone? Was there a time when the census was only that, just a count and not a window into our lives for bureaucratic Peeping Toms? . . .

Today's Feds continue fervent[ly] in their fanaticism for the census, so much so that you'd think they lack computers, the IRS [Internal Revenue Service], FISA's [Foreign Intelligence Surveillance Act of 1978] warrantless wiretaps, "pen/trap devices," black boxes at compliant ISPs [Internet service providers], and the myriad bureaucracies that monitor all we say and do. Why? When the Feds already know the answers to their infernal questions, why bother asking us?

Becky Akers,
"Year of the Rat—I Mean Census," Campaign for Liberty,
February 2, 2010. http://campaignforliberty.com.

Another concern with this intrusive questionnaire is that it signifies yet another inroad into the establishment of a permanent surveillance state. Everywhere we look these days, we are either being watched, taxed or some bureaucrat is placing another bit of information in our government files. Now with the American Community Survey, the federal bureaucracy is thrusting its expansive tentacles toward us in an attempt to invade every aspect of our lives.

This survey also hints at a dangerous wedding of governmental and corporate interests—a merger that inevitably results in personal data collected on hundreds of millions of Americans being shared with private corporations. Needless to say, with the [Barack] Obama administration poised to hire an additional one million census workers, data collecting on American citizens will be intensified over the next several years.

The True Purpose of a Census

Clearly, this is not what the Founders intended. As Article I of the U.S. Constitution makes plain, the census is to be taken every ten years for the sole purpose of congressional redistricting. The Founders envisioned a simple head count of the number of people living in a given area so that numerically equal congressional districts could be maintained. There is no way that the Founders would have authorized the federal government to continuously demand, under penalty of law, such detailed information from the American people.

However, the Founders did not anticipate the massive and meddlesome federal bureaucracy we have today or the daily onslaught of media images and governmental scare tactics designed to keep the modern American distracted and submissive. Sadly, most Americans do not seem to care that their freedoms are being whittled away or they see no point in resistance. Either way, the reaction is the same: They submit to virtually every government demand, including the highly intrusive and patently unconstitutional American Community Survey.

Thankfully, there are still some Americans out there who value freedom and recognize that it is time to stand up and fight back using whatever peaceful, nonviolent means are available to them. As Beth concludes in her e-mail to me:

> As an American loyal to my country, we have no choice but to stand against this unethical intrusion into our lives. I have called and written to many people. No response. No one seems to be listening. No one seems to care. I intend to vote for those who do care.

| "We are constitutionally justified in tell-
ing the federal government 'None of
your business' for all [census] questions
not needed for a head count."

The Census Has Overstepped
Its Constitutional Bounds

Steven Yates

*Steven Yates is an adjunct philosophy professor at the University
of South Carolina Upstate and the author of* Civil Wrongs:
What Went Wrong with Affirmative Action *and* Worldviews:
Christian Theism vs. Modern Materialism. *He is an advocate
of limited government and, in the following viewpoint, Yates argues that the census was devised under the US Constitution as a
means to count citizens to determine representation in congressional districts. He contends that census questions that go beyond
the function of a head count are unconstitutional and should be
opposed by Americans who value their privacy.*

As you read, consider the following questions:

1. According to Yates, who is the only member of Congress
   to vote "no" against the 2010 census as prepared by the
   Department of Commerce?

2. In what part of the US Constitution does Yates say the term "census" is used?

3. Why is Yates suspicious of the government's claim that 2010 census data will not be made available to agencies beyond the Census Bureau?

By now, you've doubtless received your Census 2010 in the mail, with that ominous message from your government on the outside envelope: *Your response is required by law.*

Every 10 years, the federal government conducts a census—typically in early spring. The federal government's conducting a census is constitutional, but in the words of [US representative from Texas] Ron Paul—who supplied the single "No" vote against the 2010 census the Department of Commerce prepared—the census "has grown far beyond what the framers of our Constitution intended."

The Census Is a Head Count

A capsule overview of the history of the census might be useful. The single constitutional use of the term *census* occurs in Article I, Sec. 9: "No Capitation, or other direct, Tax shall be laid, unless in proportion to the Census or enumeration herein before directed to be taken." In this case, the census is an enumeration, *that's all.* Article I, Sec. 2 had stated: "The actual Enumeration shall be made within three Years after the first Meeting of the Congress of the United States, and within every subsequent Term of ten Years, in such Manner as they shall by Law direct."

The first census was in 1790. Its purpose was a head count. This was to apportion congressional seats among the various states. But the Constitution only briefly limited government. The 1810 census began collecting information on housing conditions, schooling, achievement of students and the economy, and so on. The amount of information on census forms continued to expand.

Constitutionalists see many census questions as invading our privacy, and as mirroring the shift to collectivism and to a government that attempts to do too much. In a column explaining his "No" vote, Dr. Paul wrote, "The invasive nature of the current census raises serious questions about how and why government will use the collected information. It also demonstrates how the federal bureaucracy consistently encourages citizens to think of themselves in terms of groups, rather than as individual Americans. The not so subtle implication is that each group, whether ethnic, religious, social, or geographic, should speak up and demand its 'fair share' of federal largesse."

This year [2010], the feds have recorded the GPS coordinates of every front door, so they can pinpoint our locations with greater accuracy than ever before. The U.S. Census Bureau assures us that the information will be locked away for 72 years, and not made available to other agencies. But as Dr. Paul notes, in the past, information from the census was used during World War II to locate Japanese Americans; it was used during the Vietnam War era to find draft evaders; it has been used by the IRS [Internal Revenue Service] to detect tax evaders.

The Questionnaire

This year's census is quite short, consisting of just 10 questions—as opposed to earlier efforts that were far more elaborate (especially the controversial, invasive "long forms"). Let's have a look at the current census.

The first question reads, "How many were living in this house, apartment, or mobile home on April 1, 2010?" That question complies with the Constitution. But it is followed up with a second question that is very much a product of our times, not those of our Founding Fathers. The second question asks, "Were there any additional people staying here April 1, 2010, that you did not include in Question 1?"

The Constitutional Purpose of the Census Is to Ask Only One Question

So now that we understand that the only proper "constitutional duty" is to simply count the people in a given area (not their address, gender, work status, ethnic background, number of toilets, etc.) then why are all these very personal and private questions asked in the first place? Why does the US Census Bureau not only ask unconstitutional and personal questions but demand that they be answered?

Gary D. Barnett,
"The Unconstitutional Census Gestapo,"
Tenth Amendment Center, January 28, 2010.
http://tenthamendmentcenter.com.

Reading that question for the first time, I wanted to pencil in, *Why is this question here? Do you not trust us taxpayers to answer Question 1 truthfully?* Is it believed we might be harboring illegal aliens? Or potential terrorists? Many federal laws and regulations are, of course, built up under the assumption that we the peons cannot be trusted.

Question 3 asks, "Is this house, apartment, or mobile home—Owned with a mortgage or loan (and *include home equity loans*)? Owned ... free and clear (without a mortgage or loan)? Rented? Occupied without payment or rent? Then Question 4 follows up: "What is your telephone number? We may call if we don't understand an answer." I cannot help but wonder how one could answer Question 3 in such a way as to require a phone call—but I suppose federal bureaucrats are easily baffled.

Question 5 demands your name. Then begin the collectivist questions. Question 6 demands your sex. Question 7 calls for your age and date of birth. Questions 8 and 9 ask, respectively, whether you are of Hispanic origin and what your race is. I suppose that if you are in this country illegally, because the country has refused to enforce its own immigration laws, they expect you to tell them. The question behind the question: Do congressional districts need some new legal gerrymandering to ensure a politically correct racial balance?

Question 10 wraps up: "Does Person 1 sometimes live or stay somewhere else?" Possible responses: in college housing, at a seasonal second residence, in a nursing home, in jail or prison.

Congressman Paul notes that we are constitutionally justified in telling the federal government "None of your business" for all questions not needed for a head count. But he also notes that "there are consequences for not submitting to the census and its intrusive questions," including "a fine of up to $5000."

> *"Most activities undertaken by the federal government have no constitutional basis. One exception is the census carried out every 10 years. . . . Alas, it appears that even this core federal function is subject to cost overruns and waste."*

The Census Is Constitutional but Costly

Tad DeHaven

In the following viewpoint, Tad DeHaven claims that the decennial census—used to count citizens for allocating representation in Congress—is a legitimate government duty under the Constitution. However, DeHaven asserts that, like other government-run operations, the census is plagued by cost overruns and an inability to meet deadlines. DeHaven is a budget analyst on federal and state budget issues for the Cato Institute, a libertarian public policy research organization.

As you read, consider the following questions:

1. As DeHaven writes, how much money was the Census Bureau awarded in 2008 to meet expected cost overruns?

2. According to the inspector general of the Department of Commerce, how much is the 2010 census expected to cost?

3. As DeHaven reports, how many employees hired by the Census Bureau never worked a day but still collected pay for training?

Most activities undertaken by the federal government have no constitutional basis. One exception is the census carried out every 10 years to determine the allocation of seats in the House of Representatives. Alas, it appears that even this core federal function is subject to cost overruns and waste, as a new report from the Department of Commerce's inspector general illustrates.

Quarterly updates of progress on the census by the inspector general were required by legislation in 2008, which gave the Census Bureau an additional $210 million "to help cover spiraling 2010 decennial costs stemming from the bureau's problematic efforts to automate major field operations, major flaws in its cost-estimating methods, and other issues."

So how are things going?

Costly Foul-Ups

The census has been forced to rush the creation of a paper-based processing system for its field staff because its original plan to equip workers with handheld computers was a boondoggle. In the world of government, "rush" means that the Census [Department] told Congress in April 2008 that it was scrapping the computers.

From a NextGov.com article at the time:

In 2006, the Census Bureau awarded a $595 million contract to Harris Corp. to develop more than 525,000 handheld computers that enumerators would use to collect data from Americans who did not send in their census forms. . . . Since awarding the contract, the project has experienced constant setbacks, including changing system requirements that led to increased costs and missed deadlines. Reports by the Government Accountability Office, the department's inspector general and MITRE Corp. all issued warnings that the hand-helds were at risk of not being ready by 2010 and may not work as planned.

According to the inspector general's report, the paper-based replacement system is also having problems:

- "We found that system development and testing have fallen substantially behind schedule, resulting in less functionality and an increased likelihood of field staff's encountering technical problems during operations."

- "Although development staff have been deployed as much as possible—working two shifts per day, extended hours, weekends and holidays—the schedule to build new functionality has not appreciably improved, and testing of already developed functionality continues to fall farther behind."

- Defects in the software have gone from 26 to 80 in the past year. As a result of the software delays and defects, the development of the training materials is 31 days behind schedule.

- As for actual system performance, "Two load tests were conducted in December 2009 to determine the network and computing capacity needed during peak operations. The first test revealed numerous performance and functional problems. Although many of these problems were alleviated for the second test, performance issues persist." *Deployment is less than five weeks away.*

Failing Quality Controls

The estimated cost of the census has increased by $3.2 billion in the last two years and is now expected to cost $14.7 billion.

The Courts Have Ruled the Census Constitutional

[A]s recently as 2000, a federal judge in Houston, Texas, held that Census questions don't violate the Constitution. U.S. District Judge Melinda Harmon dismissed the complaint of five plaintiffs who claimed that the Census violated their constitutional rights. Regarding the Fourth Amendment specifically, she noted that the Census questions didn't involve uninvited entry into anyone's home, and that the information was being sought for reasonable and legitimate government purposes.

Brooks Jackson,
"Census Nonsense," FactCheck.org,
March 18, 2010. www.factcheck.org.

The inspector general's take on cost overruns at early local census offices (ELCOs) speaks for itself:

These wide variances between budgeted and actual costs do not generate confidence in the Census Bureau's budgeting and cost-containment processes for large-scale field operations.

Among the findings:

- "For production, 49 of 151 ELCOs (32 percent) exceeded their wage budgets and 75 (50 percent) exceeded their mileage budgets."

- "The ELCOs' production wage costs were 45–186 percent of their budgets and for production mileage they were less than one percent to 250 percent of their budgets."

- "For quality control, 124 of 151 ELCOs (82 percent) exceeded both their wage and mileage budgets."

- "For the quality control phase of the operation, ELCOs' wage costs were 68–439 percent of their budgets and for mileage were less than one percent to 878 percent of their budgets."

That's some quality control.
As for government efficiency:

During Address Canvassing, 15,263 employees received training but worked for less than a single day or did not work at all. Of these employees, 10,235 did not work at all but earned approximately $3.4 million for attending training. An additional 5,028 employees completed training, at a cost of $2.2 million in wages, but worked for less than a single day.

Looking at how the federal government is bungling a core constitutional function, it's amazing that we let it meddle in housing, energy, health care, and thousands of other activities the Founders didn't envision it doing.

> "History offers good reason for worrying about the misuse of [census] information."

National Censuses Have Been a Source of Controversy Throughout History

The Economist

The Economist is a British news journal that forgoes author by-lines so that the magazine speaks with a unified voice. In the following viewpoint, the unnamed author provides a history of census taking in various nations. The author claims censuses have been used to determine taxation, government representation, revenue sharing, and ethnic cleansing, and each has borne its share of difficulties. For example, while many people favor censuses for apportioning political representation, others fear censuses for dividing populations along religious or racial lines. Thus, the Economist argues that censuses are not neutral head counts but tools for governments to acquire data that can be as easily misused as properly utilized.

The Economist, "Census Sensitivity," vol. 385, no. 8560, December 22, 2007, pp. 97–99. Copyright © 2007 by The Economist. All rights reserved. Reproduced with permission.

As you read, consider the following questions:

1. According to the author, what country initiated the first constitutionally mandated census?

2. As the *Economist* reports, what kinds of questions will supposedly be excluded from the proposed 2011 census in unified Germany, and what is the reasoning behind this decision?

3. As the author states, what reason did the British government give for not including a question about sexual orientation on its 2011 census?

"Go, number Israel from Beersheba even to Dan; and bring the number of them to me, that I may know it." It was not the first census described in the Bible, nor the last, nor yet the most renowned. But for reasons that are obscure, King David's order to Joab, the commander of his army, went against God's will and both men knew it. The count was carried out all the same, and was followed by a heavy punishment: 70,000 Israelites died of the plague before the Lord relented and accepted burnt offerings as a token of David's repentance.

Taking a census thus came to be known as the sin of David, and was long regarded as best avoided. In 1634 Governor John Winthrop of the Massachusetts Bay Colony estimated the local population rather than counting it exactly, telling a correspondent: "David's example stickes somewhat with us." And when a Census Bill was debated in Britain in 1753, Matthew Ridley, the member of Parliament (MP) for Newcastle, gave a speech saying that there was among the people "such a violent spirit of opposition to this Bill, that if it be passed into a law, there is a great reason to fear, they will in many places oppose the execution of it in riotous manner."

The Purpose of Censuses

But nobody needed David's dreadful example to persuade them that censuses were a bad idea. From the point of view of those being enumerated, nothing good could come of being counted. The usual reasons for wanting the numbers were war and taxes. From the sovereign's point of view, such information was crucial: the decision to go to war could be taken only once it was known how many men could be conscripted and how much money levied. So the results were highly sensitive, and an enemy country's numbers would be useful when deciding whether attacking it was prudent, and conquering it worthwhile. The results of a Swedish census in the mid-1700s appear to have been made a state secret because of such fears.

But at the same time men were becoming enamoured of numbers and taking to counting as a way of answering pressing questions of their own. Following the London plague of 1603, weekly Bills of Mortality began to be published, listing all the deaths in the city and, from 1629, their causes. According to John Graunt, whose 90-page book interpreting and drawing conclusions from these bills is generally regarded as the earliest statistical analysis, they were used by the rich to "judge of the necessity of their removall" and by tradesmen to "conjecture what doings they were like to have". And in 1731 Benjamin Franklin published in the *Pennsylvania Gazette*, the newspaper he edited at the time, an account of all the ships that entered and left the big northern colonial ports, together with their destinations, so that the reader could "Make some Judgment of the different Share each Colony possesses of the several Branches of Trade".

It was revolution that renewed the impetus for rulers to count their people. The American war of independence brought a new nation into being, and it was not only one that was made up of separate states, each keen to get full credit for its relative size, but also one whose population was on the move. In order to decide how many representatives each state should send to the new Congress, there was only one thing for it: their populations would have to be counted, and that count would have to be repeated regularly.

Regularizing the Census in America

America's first census was carried out in 1790, and it was groundbreaking in many ways. It was the first to be mandated in any country's constitution. It was also the occasion for America's first presidential veto, exercised by George Washington on the advice of Thomas Jefferson, whom he had asked to examine the proposals for sharing out congressional seats between the states. Jefferson—a man so fond of enumeration that he once wrote to a friend that he had "ten and one-half grandchildren, and two and three-fourths great-grandchildren", and that "these fractions will ere long become units"—criticised them for being unclear about how this "apportionment" was to be carried out. He advised Washington that a completely unambiguous method should be chosen and enshrined in legislation.

The fact that this thriving new nation counted its citizens without provoking divine retribution may have given courage to other Christian countries. Over the following decade Denmark, England, the Netherlands, Norway and Sweden all instigated regular censuses of their own.

Patterns and Predictions

People started finding the sorts of patterns in the resulting data—life expectancies, crime rates, causes of death, and the mix of religions and races—that are now part of our familiar mental furniture. In the 1800s, for instance, two French statisticians, André-Michel Guerry and Adolphe Quetelet, analysed the tables of crimes against individuals and property that had recently started to be published. They were astonished by the hitherto-unsuspected regularities they found. Guerry was particularly struck by the fact that the method by which someone committed suicide could be predicted from his age. The author of an English commentary on his work described his findings thus: "The young hang themselves; arrived at a maturer age they usually blow out their brains; as they get old they recur again to the juvenile practice of suspension."

Quetelet was equally amazed by the regularity with which the various types of crime were committed. "We can enumerate in advance", he wrote, "how many individuals will stain their hands in the blood of their fellows, how many will be forgers, how many will be poisoners, almost as we can enumerate in advance the births and deaths that should occur." Such regularities, he claimed, left no role for free will in human affairs. "Society prepares the crime", he wrote in 1832, "and the guilty person is only the instrument."

Opposition to this line of thinking came from Charles Dickens, who loathed all arguments based on numbers and averages, charging that they were used to legitimise indifference to other people's suffering. His strongest broadside against those who thought that counting people was a good way to answer social questions came in his novel *Hard Times*. When Tom, the hard-hearted Gradgrind's son, is found to be a thief, he uses his father's statistical determinism to shrug off responsibility. "So many people, out of so many, will be dishonest. I have heard you talk, a hundred times, of its being a law. How can *I* help laws? You have comforted others with such things, father. Comfort yourself!"

The future, though, belonged to those like another ardent social reformer, Dickens's near-contemporary, Florence Nightingale. Best remembered for nursing wounded soldiers in the Crimean War, her sanitary reforms were based on meticulous records of hospital admissions, illnesses, treatments and outcomes. Rather than painting moving pen-portraits of soldiers left to rot on stinking, louse-ridden pallets in a hospital built on an open sewer—as Dickens would no doubt have done— she used death rates to campaign, successfully, for change.

Nowadays, a census is part of the standard equipment of a functioning state. In 1995 the UN [United Nations] called for all member nations to hold a census in the following decade.

Yet counting people remains a sensitive business for two reasons, connected with the ambiguous character of government. Where government is oppressive, people want to keep out of censuses, lest information they provide is misused. Where government provides, people want to be in censuses, and to boost their numbers, in order to claim a larger share of the goodies.

Questions of Race and Religion Prompt Concerns of Misused Data

History offers good reason for worrying about the misuse of information. The Nazis used population records to round up Jews into concentration camps. As a result, Germans are still prickly about being counted. When in the 1980s their government added new questions to the census, there was a public outcry and the constitutional court struck it down on the grounds that it conflicted with a "fundamental right to informational self-determination". Although the country is planning a census in 2011—its first since reunification—it will not be a full count, but only a sample. Respondents' surnames will be deleted as soon as possible and all data that could identify an individual will be erased once statisticians have finished with them. Questions on race and religion will not be included.

Fears that the data might be used for purposes other than the declared ones may have undermined China's most recent census in 2000. This involved 6m [million] enumerators visiting around 350m households in just ten days. They asked some rather personal questions, such as "How much did you pay for your home?" and "How often do you wash?" But it was the standard ones about the number of residents in each household and their sex and age that provoked the most anxiety. The government wanted to find out whether the country's gender imbalance was primarily due to the abortion and infanticide of females, or whether many of the missing girls were in fact alive and being concealed. To encourage parents to register over-quota children, it reduced the penalties for anyone found to have flouted the one-child law. Some also contend that large numbers of peasants who migrated illegally to the big cities will have hidden from the enumerators, and that there may be as many as 100m uncounted Chinese on top of the 1.3 billion the census found.

It isn't just oppressive governments that misuse information. In early 2007 researchers found proof of what had long been suspected: that during the Second World War the American Census Bureau had played a part in the internment of Japanese-Americans by passing some of their names and addresses to the Secret Service.

Censuses and Government Funding

In autocracies, people try to keep out of censuses. In democracies, by contrast, they want to be in them, for censuses mean numbers, and numbers mean money and power. The American census, for example, determines how around $200 billion a year of federal funds is shared out, for everything from education and welfare to highways. Such rich pickings mean that censuses are well worth fighting over.

Although Jefferson ensured the American states could not squabble about the formula used for apportionment, he could not have predicted the partisan rows about how to deal with undercounting. No census counts everyone, and the uncounted are not drawn uniformly from all walks of life. The poor, the homeless, immigrants and ethnic minorities are missed more often. The 1990 census is thought to have missed one Native American in eight.

The statisticians' solution is to follow each census with a quality check, surveying representative areas to create a picture of those overlooked in the full count and correcting the figures accordingly. Perhaps unsurprisingly, in light of the profile of those most likely to be missed, Democrats find the intellectual arguments in favour of such adjustment more compelling than Republicans do. Before the census in 2000, the Supreme Court ruled that sampling-adjusted figures could not be used for apportioning congressional seats. But the row over whether they should be used to share out cash raged until 2001, when the Census Bureau finally declared the raw figures good enough to stand unaltered.

In Britain the 2001 census was corrected using such sampling techniques, but some areas still complain that they are being undercounted. In the decade between censuses, the national statistical office updates the figures with estimates of external and internal migration. Some towns with lots of foreigners are convinced that large chunks of their population are being overlooked, losing them millions of pounds of government money. The MP [member of Parliament] for Slough, a town to the west of London full of Poles, poetically told Parliament in January that the increasing "amount of shit that goes through our local sewers" was evidence that her constituency was being sold short.

Some groups are begging to be counted because they hope to prove their importance and increase their influence with government. Church leaders in Britain were gratified when the 2001 census, the first to ask about religion, found that 70% of the population identified themselves as Christian. They reckoned this was a large enough majority to justify their religion's special place in state-run education. Whether the figures bear the weight that has been put on them is, however, questionable. Church attendance figures suggest that few of these self-identified Christians attend services more than once a year, or indeed at all. And the irreverence with which some respondents treated the question can be judged by the 390,000 people—0.7% of the population—who answered it by claiming to be Jedi.

Dashed hopes of gaining a higher profile caused despondency among gay and lesbian groups when it was decided not to add a question about sexual orientation to Britain's next census, to be held in 2011. Government statisticians were keen, but they were stymied by the difficulties of phrasing a question that would neither offend people nor leave them in the dark about what was being asked. They were mindful of the reaction to a question on self-perceived sexual identity in a recent survey by the Metropolitan Police. The most common query it provoked from respondents was: "What's heterosexuality?"

Censuses Can Bring Shares of Money and Power

That British gays wanted to stand up and be counted says much for national tolerance. It is hard to imagine the same happening in Nigeria. There, the dispute is about who will get the oil money. The country has not had an uncontested census since gaining its independence in 1960. Civil war and poorly trained enumerators have been formidable obstacles to a reliable count. The most recent census, in 2006, omitted questions about religion and tribe following demands from leaders in the largely Muslim north. Christians in the south, who believe they have been undercounted in the past, threatened a boycott unless the questions were asked. The census found 140m people: 75m in the oil-poor north and 65m in the revenue-poor south. Politicians in the north endorsed the figures; those in the south did not.

In India, the arguments are not about money, but about a different sort of resource: the jobs and university places handed out under the government's affirmative-action programme. Many *dalits*, or untouchables, have tried to escape the discrimination they face in Hinduism by converting to Christianity or Islam. But this means no longer being eligible for the programme—a restriction on religious freedom, say some, and indeed court challenges are wending their way through the system. Rather than being neutral in this dispute,

Dislike of the Census Bureau Throughout History

The Census Bureau serves the public but also has a deeply technocratic corporate culture, which explains why it often has difficulty communicating with the public. This fact helps explain how bureau staff could make a special exception to release data to a law enforcement agency, then act surprised when people got upset about it. The special tabulation for Homeland Security wasn't an act of malice. It was an act of obtuseness.

The bureau's cluelessness may also help explain why suspicion and politics have always dogged the census. In 1860, *The Saturday Evening Post* portrayed an enumerator as a buffoon who barges into the family parlor and sends everyone into a tizzy by asking "how many of ye is deaf, dumb, blind, insane, and idiotic—how many convicts there is in the family—what all your ages are, especially the old woman and the young ladies—and how many dollars the old gentleman is worth!" In 1920, southern congressmen blocked reapportionment for 10 years when the numbers showed rapid urban growth at the expense of rural areas. Over the last 30 years, various plans to make the census more accurate by statistically adjusting it have been kicked through the halls of Congress; the Supreme Court said in 1999 that adjusted numbers could not be used for legislative reapportionment without the approval of Congress, and in 2010, the bureau didn't even raise the issue.

Brad Edmondson, "Every Last One:
A Guy with a Weakness for Demography Goes Door to Door
for the Census and Discovers What a Democracy Is Made Of,"
American Scholar, vol. 79, no. 4, Autumn 2010.

the census form took sides by allowing respondents to indicate their caste as *dalit* only if they claimed to be Hindu, Sikh or Buddhist.

The shakier the state, the fiercer the rows about censuses, for numbers affect how power is distributed. In Iraqi Kurdistan, for instance, a census due to happen in 2007 was delayed. It was intended to correct figures distorted by Saddam Hussein's "Arabisation" programme, which forced many Kurds to leave and others to declare themselves Arab. If and when an Iraqi census happens, it will not only give a truer picture of the ethnic mix in a contested region, but will also have consequences for billions of dollars in oil revenues.

Lebanon has not held a census since 1932, when it counted the number of adherents to various religions in order to share out power under a system known as confessionalism. Since that time its demography has changed and the politically favoured Christians are now believed to be in a minority. Plenty of powerful people are keen to keep that quiet, so the prospects for a new official count are dim.

Unwelcome Facts from Census Data

Counting can be even more dangerous than being counted. In 1936 Stalin told his officials that the following year's census would find a total population of 170m—a figure that took no account of his slaughter of millions in famines and purges. But the enumerators found only 162m people, and also revealed other unwelcome facts, including that nearly half the population of this avowedly atheist country was religious. So Stalin denounced the count as a "wrecker's census" and had the census takers either imprisoned or shot. A new count in 1939 came up with a similar total, but this time officials wisely classified the results and gave Stalin his figure of 170m.

That Stalin insisted on this charade is a backhanded testimony to the way counting introduces people to themselves. "The interest and significance of the census for the community lie in this," wrote Leo Tolstoy of the Moscow census of 1882: "that it furnishes it with a mirror into which, willy nilly, the whole community, and each one of us, gaze." The faces that look back can surprise us still.

> *"Given the existence of the [American Community Survey], those now waging a battle over sampling vs. enumeration are truly guilty of fighting today's war with yesterday's weapons."*

Controversy Concerning the Census Stems from Partisan Politics

Morley Winograd

Morley Winograd is a fellow with NDN, a think tank examining questions of demography and geopolitics. He is also a member of the New Policy Institute and president and chief executive officer of Morwin Inc., a government reform consulting company. In the following viewpoint, Winograd argues that political parties have used the census to fit their agendas. As he recounts, Democrats have been accused of using sampling methods to ensure that minority interests were foregrounded in federal funding initiatives. Winograd asserts that Republicans have argued against sampling in hopes that census data would be utilized only for representational redistricting based on head counts. Winograd sees the American Community Survey—a more detailed survey sent to millions of Americans each year—as a better census tool. Though not free of political partisanship, the survey seems to accurately track population while providing information necessary for federal and state funding decisions, Winograd attests.

As you read, consider the following questions:

1. As Winograd reports, which former Speaker of the House of Representatives argued that Democrats in 2000 advocated sampling techniques (in addition to census data) to shift political representation in Congress?
2. What did the President Bill Clinton White House suggest the government establish to make the 2000 census bipartisan, according to the author?
3. How did the Clinton White House hope to gain Republican support for the continued use of the American Community Survey, in Winograd's view?

The announcement last week [late February 2009] that Congressional Black Caucus members plan to press President Barack Obama to keep the 2010 census under White House supervision, even if the former Democratic governor of Washington, Gary Locke, is confirmed as Commerce Secretary, brought back memories of a movie I'd seen before—a bad movie.

The statement came from U.S. Rep. William Lacy Clay, D-Mo., the caucus's leading voice on the census, and chairman of the House Oversight and Government Reform [Committee] panel, which has jurisdiction over the decennial count. His assertion that the White House needs "to be hands-on, very much involved in selecting the new census director as well as being actively involved and interested in the full and accurate count," suggests that the partisan gap about what the census should accomplish is no closer to being closed than it was 10 years ago when we last undertook the constitutionally mandated exercise in counting everyone living in America.

The gap was so big last time that it helped bring about the complete shutdown of the United States government.

Fears of Minority Over-Representation

When Newt Gingrich became Speaker of the House, he decided, in his own paranoid way, that Bill Clinton and the Democrats would use their executive authority to produce a biased census whose overcount of minorities would shift, in his opinion, 24 House seats from the Republicans to the Democrats after the 2000 census. Of course, it was ludicrous to think such an outcome would occur, since legislative boundaries are drawn by the party in power in each state. Whatever numbers the census produces in our decennial exercise can be manipulated to produce any outcome each state's ruling party desires, as U.S. Rep. Tom DeLay and his Texas Republican cronies proved a few years ago. Nevertheless, Gingrich was determined to use the congressional appropriations process to undercut any attempt by the Democrats to overstate minority populations in several states.

The method by which this nefarious plot was to be carried out, in the Republican Party's opinion, was by the use of a large sample of Americans to be surveyed at the same time as the actual count, or enumeration, required by the Constitution, was taking place. In response to concerns about previous census inaccuracies—both overcounts and undercounts—the National Academy of Sciences had recommended that the Census Bureau use survey sampling techniques to validate not just the overall count but the individual demographic subgroups that the census's enumeration process would identify. But this was a hugely expensive undertaking. To gain statistical accuracy, about 1.3 million Americans would have to respond to a lengthy survey that would cost about half a billion dollars to execute. And it was this expenditure that Gingrich refused to appropriate. When he and Clinton came to the ultimate showdown on funding the government, Gingrich blinked.

As part of the budget settlement that reopened the government after the shutdown, Clinton forced him to reinstate funding for the sample survey. But despite having established the primacy of the White House in the conduct of the census, matters actually got worse for a while. When I became director of the National Partnership for Reinventing Government (NPR) under Vice President Al Gore, I was asked to monitor the implementation of the census to be sure it was done as effectively and as efficiently as possible. But the first idea on how to accomplish that came straight out of the same White House partisan playbook that is now being invoked by the Congressional Black Caucus.

In order to assure that the process was "bipartisan," it was suggested that a commission be established made up of equal numbers of Republicans and Democrats who would oversee the activity on behalf of the Congress. Since the commission was to be equally divided, the Clinton White House wanted to make sure that only the most partisan Democrats—those who would never concede an inch to their Republican counterparts on issues such as funding and methodology—were selected. Names like Harold Ickes, Supervisor Gloria Molina, and Congresswoman Maxine Waters were discussed as representative of the type of Democrat who would make sure the use of sampling to confirm the accuracy of the count was preserved. Fortunately, thanks to the eloquence of Rob Shapiro, the undersecretary for the Department of Commerce who had the actual authority to supervise the census, cooler heads in the vice president's office were able to prevail over their White House counterparts, and the commission notion was abandoned.

From Sampling to Eliminating the Long-Form Census

But that didn't stop the two parties from continuing their warfare over the value of a sample supplemented census vs. a straight enumeration. Republicans sued the Census Bureau in federal court, demanding that only the actual count of residents as provided in the Constitution be used for any congressional redistricting by the states. The Federal Appeals court dismissed the Republican lawsuit as none of the court's business. Foreshadowing the outcome of *Bush v. Gore* in 2000, the Supreme Court surprisingly took up the case and overturned the appeals court ruling. As a result, all subsequent redistricting efforts have used only the enumeration count from the 2000 census. On the other hand, formulas used to allocate federal funds based on population characteristics were unaffected by the ruling and could have used the sampling process, had it not met an untimely and unnecessary death.

As soon as George W. Bush was elected and the incredibly professional director of the Census Bureau, Ken Prewitt, was removed from office, the Commerce Department's new partisan secretary, Donald Evans, determined that the sample that had been prepared over the strong objections of congressional Republicans was not usable. Sampling, as originally conceived, was never implemented, and the country ended up relying on a very strong effort to count households and those living in them for its 2000 census. This method tends to overcount families with two houses, who respond to the census form at both of their addresses, and college students who generally answer the form from their dorm room while their parents report them as still in their household back home. And, of course, it tends to undercount less affluent populations with fewer physical ties to a specific dwelling, particularly Native Americans, and to some degree Hispanics and African Americans.

Despite these problems, a sampling approach could not be used to help correct inaccuracies in this year's census, even if [former White House chief of staff to Barack Obama] Rahm Emanuel himself were to oversee it. We are too far along in the process to recreate it. There is, however, a substitute available that should alleviate the concerns of all but the most stubborn partisans on both sides of the issue. Under the Gore reinvention initiative, the Census Bureau conceived of a concept now known as the American Community Survey [ACS]. It was designed to survey a vast quantity of households over time to acquire the kind of detailed demographic data that was usually obtained from the subset of the population, about one in 10, who were asked to complete the "long form" of the census questionnaire every 10 years. Republicans hated this form and the type of questions it asked; they saw it as an unlawful intrusion on the privacy of families by the federal government. Those of us in charge of reinventing the federal government thought the ACS could be a much more scientific and efficient way of collecting this essential data, but our challenge was to keep it from becoming a political football in the partisan warfare over the census.

Finally, it was agreed that the Clinton administration budget proposals would include a continuing increase in funds for the ACS. In order to garner Republican support, ACS would be justified as a way to eliminate the long form by 2010. The budget request was forwarded by the head of ACS directly to the vice president's office, which made it a priority each year, but which never publicly acknowledged any interest in the concept. The ruse worked and the project became a reality. The long form will not be used in the upcoming census because the ACS has gathered, over time, sufficient data on the demographic details of America's population as to make it unnecessary.

Given the existence of the ACS, those now waging a battle over sampling vs. enumeration are truly guilty of fighting today's war with yesterday's weapons. In this new era, those who have a legitimate interest in as complete and accurate a census as possible should instead direct their efforts to the neighborhoods where the accuracy of the count will actually be determined. During the last count, the Census Bureau formed hundreds of thousands of partnerships with community groups interested in making sure that everyone they knew got counted. Today, these programs, as well as projects such as former Detroit mayor Dennis Archer's "Nosy Neighbors" campaign, are the best way to ensure an accurate outcome.

The responsibility for America's next census does not and should not rest with the White House. But President Obama's experience does offer some direction: neighborhood organizing is key. Let's hope that community leaders will follow the advice to "pick yourself up and dust yourself off" . . . and undertake the huge task of ensuring that every person is present and accounted for in America's next census.

Periodical Bibliography

The following articles have been selected to supplement the diverse views presented in this chapter.

Margo Anderson	"An Enumeration of the Population: A History of the American Census," *Insights on Law & Society*, Winter 2010.
John S. Baker and Elliott Stonecipher	"Our Unconstitutional Census," *Wall Street Journal*, August 10, 2009.
Kevin Chappell	"Stand Up and Be Counted," *Ebony*, March 2010.
Jill Colvin	"Down for the Count," *First Things*, April 2010.
Brad Edmondson	"Every Last One: A Guy with a Weakness for Demography Goes Door-to-Door for the Census and Discovers What a Democracy Is Made Of," *American Scholar*, September 2010.
Nancy Gibbs	"The U.S. Census: Why Our Numbers Matter," *Time*, April 5, 2010.
Terence P. Jeffrey	"The 2010 Census Being Used to Sell the Welfare State," *Human Events*, April 20, 2009.
Jack Kenny	"Counting the Cost of the Census," *New American*, March 3, 2009.
Elinor Tatum	"How Will We Be Counted or Will We Be Counted Out?," *New York Amsterdam News*, March 26–April 1, 2009.
USA Today	"Debate on Decennial Head Count Our View: Census Is a Simple Civic Duty, Not a Government Inquisition," March 19, 2010.
Martha Zoller	"Obama Administration Makes Power Grab on Census," *Human Events*, February 16, 2009.

OPPOSING VIEWPOINTS® SERIES

CHAPTER 2

Does the US Census Accurately Represent the Country's Population?

Chapter Preface

According to the US Census Bureau, 74 percent of households participated in the 2010 census. That's a considerable increase from 2000 and 1990, the two previous decennial censuses that yielded 67 percent and 61 percent respectively. The federal government's $340 million promotional campaign may have boosted census returns, but while the high percentage was a promising show for the country, some states still experienced a decline in participation.

According to an April 26, 2010, *USA Today* article, the mail returns of the census dropped steeply (that is, by 3 percent or more) from 2000 to 2010 in Alaska, California, Colorado, Louisiana, Montana, Nebraska, New Mexico, North Dakota, Oklahoma, South Dakota, West Virginia, Wisconsin, and Wyoming (which experienced the largest decrease of all the states at 6 percent). Observers may debate which demographics will not reap the benefits because of poor census returns, but some are focused instead on the causes of the lack of participation and the likelihood of remedying disparities in the future.

In an April 16, 2010, column, Daniel Stone of *Newsweek* claimed that right-wing partisanship might have prevented some citizens from mailing in their 2010 forms. He points to political commentator Glenn Beck and Congresswoman Michele Bachmann as Republican spokespersons who vowed either not to participate in the census or attempted to convince their followers "that the Obama administration will try to use the information gathered through the census for nefarious purposes." These boycott campaigns may indeed have had some effect given that five out of the thirteen "low participation" states skewed toward the Democratic Party based on the retrieved census data.

While ideology might have been a factor for some, others did not participate due to fear of identity theft scams or of immigration concerns (such as language barriers or fear of deportation). Yet, the most enduring reason after all these years is accessibility. Some households are simply hard to find. Eric Aasen of the *Dallas Morning News* believes that certain towns in Texas, due to their rural nature, will seldom achieve an adequate participation rate. In a March 30, 2010, piece posted on the Texas Cable News website, he asserts that the challenge is nationwide: "To help locate hard-to-find people in rural America, the [US Census] Bureau has sent workers on horseback in Texas, on snowmobiles in Maine and by plane to remote parts of Alaska." In remote parts of West Virginia, New Mexico, Alaska, and Louisiana, census participation is among the lowest in the nation, and the census takers struggle to reach citizens by whatever means are at their disposal.

Expanding the reach of the census and the return rate of census documents remains the chief goal of the Census Bureau. In the following chapter, various experts comment on the efficacy in accounting for minorities, prisoners, college students, and other demographics within the purview of the census. As always, the accuracy of the count determines who will be represented in America's cultural and political landscape.

> "The Census Bureau, which needs
> Americans to cooperate with its survey,
> is understandably leery about privacy
> breaches."

Census Bureau Obscured Personal Data—Too Well, Some Say

Carl Bialik

In the following viewpoint, Wall Street Journal writer Carl Bialik reports that attempts to protect the privacy of US census respondents may be obscuring statistics generated from the data. Bialik explains that the Census Bureau commonly rounds off or averages data and even figuratively transplants respondents from one state to another in routine attempts to keep the identity of census takers protected. Because statisticians who rely on census data are concerned that this will undermine their projects and skew their findings, the government is looking into ways to improve the integrity of the data released, Bialik maintains.

As you read, consider the following questions:

1. According to the author, why is the decennial census not affected by the errors occurring in microdata samples?

2. As Bialak reports, what organization released a paper in early 2010 disclosing the fact that privacy protections were skewing statistical outcomes from microdata samples?

3. What is the "broader worry" raised by the microdata errors, in Bialak's view?

Errors in some U.S. Census Bureau data are sending researchers inside and outside government scrambling to check whether some key findings need to be reassessed.

After the Census Bureau compiles overall counts in its decennial population surveys and other studies, it releases additional details about respondents to outside researchers. But in order to protect respondents' privacy, the bureau masks some of the personal information in these so-called microdata.

Now, a study has found that the agency went too far hiding individual identities, introducing errors that might lead economists and demographers astray.

By relying on the microdata, researchers would have found, for example, evidence of a steep drop-off in marriage rates for women at age 65, or of a big rise in the proportion of women in their early 70s who are working—both false conclusions.

The anomalies highlight how vulnerable research is to potential problems with underlying numbers supplied by other sources, even when the source is the federal government. And they illustrate how tricky it can be to balance privacy with accuracy.

The Census Bureau, which needs Americans to cooperate with its survey, is understandably leery about privacy breaches.

"We have this tension in our lives," says Robert M. Groves, director of the Census Bureau. "We want to preserve confidentiality, and we want to maximize utility of our data. This tension is inherent in everything we do. We're always talking about it."

No decennial census—the big survey that is used to allot congressional seats and allocate government spending—is affected by the problems, because the once-a-decade counts contain only aggregated data. The agency publishes breakdowns by age, gender, race and other factors, but the subgroups are so large that in most cases no one respondent can be identified.

Many researchers, though, want to dig deeper into the wealth of information collected by the census every 10 years, as well as in the monthly American Community Survey and Current Population Survey. To help them, the bureau releases microdata, which are a subset of all survey responses. Thus researchers can study the income of, say, married, 65-year-old women in North Dakota.

But slicing the data so thinly raises privacy concerns. Suppose there is only one 65-year-old married woman attending college in North Dakota, and that her response was released by the Census Bureau. Then researchers would know everything else she told the agency, including, perhaps, her income and her parents' birthplace.

To protect the privacy of such unusual individuals and households, the government manipulates data, using several techniques that were described in a 2005 Census Bureau paper. Numbers are rounded, so incomes of $80,600 and $81,400 would both be recorded as $81,000. What statisticians refer to as "noise" is added to some ages—a year or two older or younger, perhaps.

Also, outlier values are averaged together, and that average is assigned to every one of those outliers. For instance, the top half percent of earners would each be assigned the average income of that wealthy subgroup, so that, say, Warren Buffett's census questionnaire can't be identified. And people with especially unique characteristics might be moved across the country, in a kind of statistical witness protection program, so that entry for the North Dakotan woman might be changed to show her living in Alabama.

When using microdata from the Census Bureau, economist Betsey Stevenson at the University of Pennsylvania's Wharton School stumbled upon what seemed like an intriguing trend: The marriage rate for women at age 65 was 50%, eight percentage points lower than at age 64. She wondered what might explain such a precipitous drop.

"Then I realized this is not a matter of women changing behavior," Prof. Stevenson says. "This is a problem with the data."

A broader look at other census data sets found similar problems, such as miscounting men and women at certain ages above 65. In a paper released this week by the National Bureau of Economic Research, Prof. Stevenson and co-authors J. Trent Alexander from the Minnesota Population Center at the University of Minnesota and Michael Davern, from the University of Chicago's National Opinion Research Center, argue that the privacy-protection techniques had introduced substantial deviations in the microdata, when compared with overall census counts.

Flawed software programming appears to be at fault. Laura Zayatz, chair of the Census Bureau's disclosure review board, says code designed to add the statistical noise to the subset of older respondents should have offset those changes with opposite adjustments made elsewhere in the data sample. This didn't happen as it should have, so that ages and other attributes were skewed.

Before the data were released in 2003, the Census Bureau's diagnostic tools flagged the problem, but it "didn't seem large enough in the judgment of our analysts to stop the release," says Dr. Groves, the Census Bureau director.

"We have some facts about you that you don't remember, some that you thought were really secret, and some that never even happened," cartoon by S. Harris, www.CartoonStock.com. Copyright © by S. Harris. Reproduction rights obtainable from www.CartoonStock.com.

Since the research by Prof. Stevenson's group emerged, the Census Bureau has been reevaluating policies on disclosure risk and diagnosing errors in data before they are released. "I'm going to ask for a very careful cracking of this code so we find out what data are possibly affected," Dr. Groves says.

Researchers elsewhere are revisiting their work to learn how it might have affected their findings. Though the Census Bureau had released notes to data users addressing some of the problems, the agency hasn't yet corrected all data sets, and some users of the microdata were unaware of the problems before this week. Representatives for the Social Security Administration and the Office of Management and Budget—agencies mentioned as heavy users of microdata in the paper—said they are checking to see if any of their findings were affected.

J. Michael Brick, a statistician at research company Westat, says the problems could alter opinion polls of older Americans that are weighted according to the microdata. "There could be some very misleading analysis," Dr. Brick says.

University of Utah sociologist Claudia Geist says that she used some of the affected data in a 2008 paper she co-wrote about geographical mobility. So far, she hasn't found any problems, but she adds, "We will continue to examine the data, because this is a wake-up call to all who use these data."

The findings raise a broader worry: that even when the numbers in microdata match the broader census, all the swapping, rounding and other adjustments made to protect privacy might obscure links researchers are examining, such as between income and marital status.

And some researchers think the agency's efforts to protect privacy might not be worth the trouble, because identity thieves and others who hunt down personal data with illicit intentions might be able to find the information elsewhere.

"There is nothing in the regular census ... data that could not be learned far more easily than by using supercomputers and data mining to try to hack into the census," says Steven Ruggles, director of the Minnesota Population Center.

> "Racial minorities and college commu-
> nities have historically been among so-
> called 'hard to call' population groups
> in America and have tended to be un-
> dercounted in the national population
> head count."

The Census Undercounts College Students

Reginald Stuart

*In the following viewpoint, Reginald Stuart, a writer for the
journal* Diverse: Issues in Higher Education, *reports that college
students are commonly underrepresented in US census data.
Stuart claims that this is because students often fail to understand that they should fill out census forms for the location they
reside while attending school. Stuart points out that some colleges and student groups are trying to encourage students to participate more because federal aid for education is based on census data. However, Stuart reports that not all colleges have made
effective partnerships with the Census Bureau to educate students about the importance of the census.*

Reginald Stuart, "Standing Up for the Count," *Diverse: Issues in Higher Education*, vol.
26, no. 26, February 4, 2010, pp. 7–8. Copyright © 2010 by *Diverse: Issues in Higher
Education*. www.DiverseEducation.com. All rights reserved. Reproduced with permission.

As you read, consider the following questions:

1. How much federal funding is apportioned to states via census statistics, according to Stuart?

2. As Stuart reports, which university developed a census video to play at halftime during winter basketball games in 2009–2010?

3. How much has the government spent on a census promotion plan to make people aware of the census and its importance, as the author explains?

When the U.S. Census Bureau begins conducting its official national population head count April 1 [2010], the outcome of its efforts will, in part, reflect how successful it has been in partnering with colleges to drum up interest among students in participating in the national head count.

Racial minorities and college communities have historically been among so-called "hard to call" population groups in America and have tended to be undercounted in the national population head count conducted by the Census Bureau once every 10 years. This year could produce the same results, absent significant outreach by the bureau and the nation's colleges and universities.

The Significance of the Head Count

"The census is perhaps the most significant decennial event occurring in America because it affects everything from the drawing of congressional districts to the flow of resources to the community," says Dr. Charlie Nelms, chancellor of North Carolina Central University [NCCU].

"If you're not counted, you're counted out," says Nelms, whose school provided the Census Bureau with computers and classroom space last fall to test job prospects. The school also gave the agency space in the school's football stadium concession area, called E-town, to distribute information about the census.

By law, the census count is used to determine how many seats in the United States House of Representatives each state gets until the next census is conducted in another 10 years. As importantly, population figures gathered by the census are used to create mathematical formulas to determine how some $450 billion in federal revenue is divided each year among the states in the form of federal aid.

A good census count means a lot for colleges and college communities that look to the federal government for all kinds of assistance, officials say, ranging from aid for tuition grants to funds for academic research and funds for area and campus safety programs.

Partnering with Colleges

NCCU was not alone in its bid to help. Tuskegee University in Alabama opened its doors last fall to census promoters who gave away census T-shirts, literature about the upcoming count and information about temporary jobs as census workers. Savannah State University in Georgia was set to send students this winter to a census summit aimed at mobilizing college students.

In Michigan, where the poor state and national economies have caused major population losses, census officials have partnered with Detroit's Wayne State University, Michigan State University and a number of area community colleges to work together to put the census on people's radars.

The University of Texas at San Antonio [UTSA], has a 15-member task force, led by the school's president, developing one of the more ambitious plans among colleges for stimulating interest and participation in the census, says John Kaulfus, associate dean of students at UTSA, a school with a large Hispanic enrollment.

UTSA has developed a census video to be played during the halftime of UTSA home basketball games this winter. It has developed census pitches for its Facebook and MySpace pages. It is making signage that will be placed on many school buses in the weeks leading up to the official April 1 count day. A traveling census van is scheduled to stop at the campus in mid-February to rev up student interest. The local message at the school's annual Rowdystock concert, set for late March, is the importance of participating in the 2010 census.

"Students don't understand they are to be counted where they are," says Kaulfus. "They assume their parents are counting them," he says. That is the wrong assumption to make, Kaulfus and census officials say, unless the student is physically living at home on April 1.

Educating Students About the Census

Still, counting college students poses its challenges.

"We have a lot of education and advocacy to do," says Laura Waldon, partnership specialist for the Census Bureau's Census on Campus campaign in the Northeast. Waldon says the Northeast census team has designed and launched a college focused website, 2010Census.gov/campus, aimed at stimulating college student interest. They are also working to get schools in the region to hold a Census Week in March to "raise student awareness," says Waldon. "It's a busy time" for students, she says, with "spring break, final exams. It's definitely a challenge."

In addition to the distractions of daily life, Waldon says other hurdles for some students may be that census forms for 2010 are not online where many students spend much of their time. Trying to remind people of the residency rules—you fill out a form with information based on where you are April 1, regardless of whether that is your permanent residence—is also a challenge, says Waldon and some school officials. Work needs to be done to get foreign students in America attending college to be sure to fill out a form on April 1, as the census seeks to determine the number of people living in the nation on that date, regardless of their homeland.

Despite its importance and a $300 million promotion campaign launched in January, not every college has been actively recruited to help get out the count.

Officials at Xavier University in New Orleans, a city still reeling from the aftermath of Hurricane Katrina, say they had brief contact with census representatives last fall and have not heard a word since about helping.

"Nobody is aware of any efforts, outreach or otherwise, to engage our campus or its students in census awareness or participation of any sort," says Xavier spokesman Warren Bell.

Bell says census officials asked Xavier last fall for space to conduct some interviews and testing and have not contacted the school since.

Several calls to Census Bureau organizers in the South about their work in the region were not returned.

> *"When the [Census Bureau] began measuring across all races and ethnicities in 1990, it found blacks, Latinos and Native Americans were all undercounted at more than double the national rate."*

The Census Undercounts Minority Groups

Kai Wright

Kai Wright is the editorial director of ColorLines, an online news site covering issues of racial justice in America. He is also a writer whose work has appeared in the Nation *and the* American Prospect. *Wright argues in the following viewpoint that minorities are typically undercounted in the US census. Using the influx of Latino immigrants to make his case, Wright claims that many undocumented immigrants resist filling in census information for fear of being deported or otherwise penalized by the government. Wright suggests that the resulting inaccurate head counts in areas heavily populated by immigrants can deprive these communities of needed government funding for health and education services.*

Kai Wright, "Counting on the Census," *The Nation*, vol. 290, no. 19, May 17, 2010, pp. 11–17. Copyright © 2010 by *The Nation*. All rights reserved. Reproduced with permission.

As you read, consider the following questions:

1. According to Wright, roughly what percentage of those living in Southwest Houston's Latino neighborhoods who were mailed census documents in 2010 filled out and returned the forms?

2. How many people does Wright say were deported in the first year of Barack Obama's presidency?

3. As Wright reports, what percentage of Houston residents surveyed in 2009 agreed that children of undocumented parents should be permitted to attend public schools?

Even though Julia DeLeon has lived in Houston for more than half her life, built a business here, raised two daughters and is now helping to rear a toddler grandson, she doesn't exist—not statistically at least. DeLeon first moved to Houston in the 1980s. When she got sick while pregnant and an emergency room attendant refused to admit her because she's not a documented resident, she retreated to Guatemala. But DeLeon couldn't stay away. Her sister had lived here and was certain the town held opportunity. So she returned with her newborn, settled in at a friend's apartment in Southwest and started rebuilding her life.

If either the 1990 or 2000 census crossed her mind amid all of this, she doesn't remember it. She wouldn't likely have participated, anyway. After all, she didn't even have a valid lease, let alone a valid visa. Standing up to be counted by federal officials wasn't high on her to-do list.

"I just make a little part in the corner where they grew up," DeLeon recalls of the apartment where she raised Evelyn DeLeon, now 21, and Sharon Garcia, 16. "I just try to find a way in the school, any program so they not just stuck in the house. Like, making the Girl Scouts, art classes, in the church—some kind of organization where they can go, and it's not costing me much and they learn something."

Now, having painstakingly built a successful house-cleaning business, DeLeon sits in her own living room and listens proudly as her daughters talk about the importance of finally "being counted" in the 2010 census. "I do it," she shrugs. "Ten years back, I was maybe afraid if they deport us—what happen with these two girls? But now, if something happen with me, it's not really a worry," she says, turning to Evelyn, who's been volunteering in an ad hoc campaign to encourage census participation in the neighborhood. "She can support now."

Minorities Undercounted

That seemingly blasé statement represents a huge victory for the Census Bureau. The DeLeon family—working-class, urban people of color—is just the sort of household the bureau has struggled to count for decades. Census statisticians discovered in 1940 that they were undercounting blacks by as much as double-digit percentages. Decade after decade, as the overall count grew more accurate, a racial gap in undercounting held firm. When the bureau began measuring across all races and ethnicities in 1990, it found blacks, Latinos and Native Americans were all undercounted at more than double the national rate.

As a result, the nation's largest metro areas have also been consistently shorted in the decennial census. The bureau keeps a list of characteristics that make it tough to enumerate a given tract: lots of renters, low household incomes, new immigrant communities, single-parent families and large populations of people of color, among others. The list informs a ranking of "hard-to-count areas" that's essentially a big-city roll call—Los Angeles County, Brooklyn, Chicago's Cook County and Houston's Harris County fill the top four spots this year [2010].

As of late April, a familiar pattern was emerging with the 2010 census. Just over 70 percent of the 134 million mailed questionnaires had been returned. Small, largely white counties in the Plains and Midwest were registering response rates of 80 percent and up. Barely half of DeLeon's neighborhood had responded, as was the case throughout Southwest Houston's densely Latino neighborhoods; Brooklyn was at just about half, Chicago at 60 percent. In May, census workers will start knocking on doors of homes that haven't replied.

The Consequences of Undercounting

The consequences of undercounting stretch far past mapping congressional districts. Decennial census numbers are used to plan things ranging from city council seats to airports and to divvy up hundreds of billions of dollars in federal support for state and local initiatives every year. In 2000 census monitors analyzed how the undercount that year would affect funding for just eight federal programs. New York City was predicted to lose a collective $847 million. Harris County looked to miss out on roughly $240 million. This loss is amplified by the fact that undercounted communities are often those most in need of government programs—Medicaid, Head Start and special education, for example—whose funds are determined by census data.

Planners fear that this year the collapsed economy will complicate things further still. Unemployment rates among blacks and Latinos are as much as a third higher than the national average. Communities with high foreclosure and job-loss rates are more likely to have families in unstable, temporary housing. It's a statistical negative feedback loop in the making.

In the past decade Washington has spent $14 billion, more than twice the cost of the 2000 census, to avoid such bleak math. Over the past year, the Census Bureau has joined local governments and community groups to mobilize hundreds of thousands of neighborhood opinion-shapers to persuade families like the DeLeons to participate. It is by far the nation's most ambitious attempt ever to enumerate itself.

But the challenges the census faces are both greater and more complex than the mechanics of a head count. Families like the DeLeons—young and brown-skinned migrants—are driving rapid demographic changes in the United States. Many of these new residents are uncertain about whether government is a source of support or a threat—the long arm behind immigration raids, detentions and record-high deportations. The answer becomes less clear as the Right stokes an increasingly polarized debate over immigration. The Tea Party's smears of the government as an intrusive, untrustworthy force are often vocalized simultaneously with the charge that government sold out "real Americans" in favor of "illegal" menaces. In October [2009], Louisiana Senator David Vitter tried adding a question about immigration status on the stripped-down 2010 census form. He hoped to spark a fight about whether undocumented residents should be enumerated at all. The Congressional Research Service countered that the Constitution clearly dictates that the census count "persons" living in the United States, not citizens. But the question Vitter sought to force is one the modern census—with its mandate of rendering a national portrait in hard, tangible numbers—cannot avoid: Who does and does not count?

Meanwhile, Tea Partyers aren't the only ones voicing distrust; it runs deep in regions like Southwest. Recent Pew Research Center polls found new immigrants articulating greater trust in government than people born here. If so, it's a complex faith in Southwest, where lived experiences like Julia DeLeon's thwarted emergency room visit often overshadow the message of city and census officials—that all residents matter. As a result, the nation may find itself unable to fulfill one of the Constitution's most basic assignments—to count the population every ten years—at a time when policy makers need the data it generates more than ever.

Young Latinos Dominate Texas

As goes Texas, so goes the nation. By far the country's fastest-growing state, Texas is gaining on California for the title of most populous. As the housing crash reversed trends in such rapid-growth states as Georgia and North Carolina, the Texas population boom appeared to continue apace in 2008 and '09. The decennial census, which takes a closer look than the bureau's yearly estimates, is expected to show this trend intensifying.

But it would be far more accurate to say that east Texas is the fastest-growing state in the nation. Rice University professor Steve Murdock was George W. Bush's last census director and has been Texas demographer for decades. He's got a state map divided into counties, with red marking those that are shrinking and blue, those that are growing fastest. The largely rural, overwhelmingly white counties in the west form a sea of blood-red. The eastern half is dominated by three massive blue blobs, each a leg of the Houston-Dallas-San Antonio triangle and each a place where whites are in the minority. Actually, Texas stopped being a majority-white state in 2004. It's one of four states, with California, Hawaii and New Mexico, the Census Bureau calls "majority-minority."

Texas's new residents are not only overwhelmingly brown; they are overwhelmingly young. Nearly half of 18- to 29-year-olds in Harris County are Latino, according to Rice University's [Kinder] Institute for Urban Research, while 70 percent of people over 60 are white. The bureau estimates that the county's Latino population grew by 40 percent between 2000 and 2008, while the white population grew less than 1 percent.

Bureau estimates show a nearly identical growth pattern for US residents overall: a young, growing population of people of color, particularly Latinos, alongside an old, plateauing population of whites. In 2000 nearly half of the residents enumerated as "Hispanic—any race" were under 25, as were 42 percent of those counted as "Non-Hispanic Black." Just 30 percent of residents who identified as "Non-Hispanic White" were under 25. The Latino population likely grew by a third between 2000 and 2008, while the white population grew by

2.5 percent—a gap that will only grow as today's youth have kids, and as their parents and grandparents die.

"The Texas of today is the United States of tomorrow," says Murdock, pointing to a national map in which states across the South and West—places with large nonwhite populations—are booming with new residents, while states in the country's middle hold flat. "Where there are diverse populations in the United States, there is population growth. Where there is less diversity, there is less growth," Murdock concludes.

This blunt fact inspires one of two reactions in America's political culture: hope or fear. To people like Angela Blanchard, who runs Houston's Neighborhood Centers, a social service agency working largely in immigrant communities, Houston is a beacon on a hill. "There's a huge entrepreneurial spirit that's fed by a massive amount of immigration. Last year we crossed the line as the most diverse city in the United States," she says, shaking her head at the fact. "No one thinks of Houston that way. But it's just amazing to live in a place where everybody's here!"

Southwest Houston certainly feels more like Queens than middle America. A four-mile stretch along the main east-west artery is packed with retail shops targeting a broad Asian community. The area has been booming steadily since the mid-1980s, recessions notwithstanding; Houston boasts 16,000 Asian-owned firms, the sixth-largest concentration in the nation as of 2002. "When I was growing up, if we saw an Asian we'd stop the car and point," jokes Glenda Joe, a Chinese-American Houston native with whom city planners have contracted to promote the census. "Now look left and right, and all you'll see is Asians—Filipino, Korean, Chinese."

Thousands of them don't exist in the official population count, however. The 2000 census tallied around 5,500 Koreans in Houston; Dongwook Yang, managing editor of the *Korean Journal*, says the city's two largest Korean churches alone have

Undercounting Hispanics

Hispanics and other minorities have historically been undercounted in the once-a-decade survey. . . .

The 2000 census counted 35,305,818 Hispanics in the United States. Hispanic groups estimate that several million more were missed. In 2007, the most recent year available, the Hispanic population had grown to an estimated 44,852,816.

Associated Press, "New Challenges Arise for Hispanics, Other Minorities in 2010 Census," March 16, 2009.

at least 3,000 members between them, and his paper's community directory includes nearly fifty more churches. "If I buy the pastors' estimation," says Yang, "it can be more than 40,000." But that sort of napkin calculation is meaningless when businesses are struggling to convince investors and would-be migrants of Houston's burgeoning Asian community. "They think about Dallas instead," Yang complains.

Immigrant Fears

The Korean undercount is infamous among city planners, too. "Houston Independent School District's statistics indicate there are at least 30,000 Koreans in HISD," scoffs Margaret Wallace, assistant director of Houston's planning department. Wallace has a map of neighborhoods where the city has struggled most to get an accurate demographic picture and where the department is targeting its 2010 effort. "We are treating this essentially as an election campaign, and we're gonna do that kind of ground campaign."

DeLeon's neighborhood sits inside a stretch of districts in Southwest Houston that feature prominently on Wallace's

map. The area's hub is Gulfton, a small, tightly packed neighborhood dominated by a handful of massive apartment com-
plexes. The area was developed in the 1960s as a convenient
suburb for young, upwardly mobile white families. A deep recession in the 1980s pushed those families out, leaving affordable housing stock for new Central American immigrants. By
the 2000 census, the neighborhood had grown by 40 percent
while white residents in the broader area had fallen by half.
The city estimates that three-quarters of Gulfton's residents
are Latino. . . .

Enrique Sapon, a church-group leader in Gulfton's Guate-
malan community, is sitting in Benito Juarez's office in
Gulfton's new city-funded community center. Juarez, a community liaison in the mayor's immigrant affairs office, spends
his days finding neighborhood surrogates like Sapon to pull in
residents for all manner of services, from prenatal health to
English classes. But all conversations lead back to one place.

"We are planning for immigration reform, and to inform
and raise the consciousness of the people," Sapon says when
asked about the census. For many in the neighborhood, the
word "government" only triggers fears about immigration
policy. "Because people don't want any more raids and families being separated because they are deported." The only
question to be answered about the census is how participating
will impact the path to citizenship.

Residents' answers vary widely but are most often rooted
in suspicion. Sapon is not terribly moved by the promises that
census information is confidential. "It's the same thing they
were saying about the Social Security and the hospitals," he
says, before citing neighborhood lore about people being deported out of hospital beds. "There have been cases." Another
rumor in Southwest is that the effort to get everyone counted
is a ploy to set up a mass deportation sweep. Others fear that
showing how many immigrants are truly here will fan public
animosity toward them. "Anyway, if they don't fill out the

form, somebody is going to come knock on the door," Sapon says of his neighbors, "so they are just praying that nothing happens." . . .

Deportation Raids Increase

Cynthia (not her real name) is being polite, but she's not terribly interested in talking, certainly not about the government's desire to know who she is and where she lives. She listens patiently as Evelyn DeLeon explains in Spanish why the ten-year census is so important. But DeLeon might as well be telling her to drink poison.

"She feels like it's some sort of trap," DeLeon says, translating Cynthia's response. "She knows that she's seen it on TV," DeLeon explains, "and that this will benefit our children so that they can be counted and get help." But that sounds like BS to Cynthia. "Whatever they say it is, she thinks it's the opposite."

Cynthia is, however, thrilled to talk about her daughter in Honduras. The proud mom holds out a cell phone picture of the 18-year-old decked out in a graduation robe. She's off to college, and Cynthia, 47, is in Houston breaking her back for $230 a week because it's contributing to her daughter's future. She figures whatever kind of help this census thing is offering, it's not likely to advance that singular goal. So it's not worth the risk of getting deported.

Her suspicions about whether and how she counts to the government would be confirmed later that night. Her closest friends, who, like her, are undocumented, were called to the airport to pick up their young son, a US citizen by birth. They had sent him home to Honduras with friends who are also citizens, but border cops wouldn't let the group back into Houston without the boy's legal guardians. When the parents arrived to claim him, they were arrested for visa violations. Separated from their son, they will be detained indefinitely and likely deported.

As the Census Bureau has flooded neighborhoods like Gulfton with its "be counted" message, the [Barack] Obama administration has ratcheted up deportations to a record high. Immigration and Customs Enforcement deported nearly 400,000 people in Obama's first year. And the president has hardened his tone on immigration; he moved from using the term "undocumented workers" on the campaign trail to "illegal immigrants" during the health care debate, when anti-immigrant rhetoric on the national stage soared.

"What's really different that wasn't there even ten years ago is this evolving anti-immigrant sentiment," says Commissioner Garcia. "We really had not felt it here as strongly as we see it on TV and around this country," she adds, "but in this past year, we're starting to see more raids."

Impact on Children

The nightmarish idea of undocumented parents being separated from their children looms over any family's daily risk calculations. Cynthia, for instance, avoids food stamps, despite her challenges buying groceries for her youngest daughter, a grade-schooler in Houston and a US citizen. "She stopped going because they were asking for way too much information, and she felt uncomfortable," DeLeon explains. That fear also means Cynthia's daughter won't be counted toward her neighborhood's elementary school or toward education grants based on census numbers. She's among nine out of ten Houston public school students who are either Latino or black.

Garcia says this is the sort of thing that makes the anti-immigrant furor so counterproductive. It's clear that new immigrants infuse a city with the entrepreneurial ethos Neighborhood Centers' Blanchard gushes about. But it's also true they are often starting from scratch in an exploitative labor market. Nearly a quarter of both Latinos and blacks lived in poverty in 2008. A Southern Education Foundation study noted earlier this year that the South's public schools are now majority-minority; three years ago the region became the first to have a majority of its students be so poor they qualify for free lunch. Those students are the future workforce.

"We're already here, and it's quite doubtful we're going to be going anywhere," Garcia lectures. "So what we need to do is work together on solving these challenges to ensure that there's not some sort of meltdown in ten years. We gotta get ready."

Rice's [Kinder] Institute for Urban Studies, which has been tracking opinions and demographics in Houston for three decades, has found an increasing number of people who disagree. Just 64 percent of people surveyed last year agreed that kids of undocumented parents should be able to go to public schools, down from 71 percent three years ago. Similarly, half of those surveyed last year wanted to deny "health and welfare services" to undocumented residents. On a question measuring opinions about a range of populations—from whites to Muslims to gays and lesbians—"undocumented immigrants" scored the worst. . . .

The census taps a conflict deep in the American psyche. Our multiple identities have long been at odds. We're a nativist country, built on immigration. The Statue of Liberty welcomes newcomers in New York Harbor, as a fence turns them away at the Texas border. Little wonder a process that quantifies this debate's futility is fraught.

The Constitution nonetheless demands it be done, and myriad government functions have come to depend on it. After decades of bitter legal and political wrangling over whether and how the bureau could use a sampling formula to fill in the undercount, bureau scientists voluntarily shelved the idea after the 2000 count. Disparate experts agreed that the formula wasn't working, though it could be figured out if politics allowed science to run its course.

The unintended result is that Congress has been backed into budgeting previously unthinkable sums for an old-fashioned tally. In 2000 that investment appeared to pay off;

the census got its first-ever paid-advertising budget, inaugurated the community partnerships that have been a definitive part of the 2010 count and beefed up staff for in-person follow-ups. All of this drove up overall response rates and helped close the racial gap.

The bureau hopes to roll that success over into this year's count. But few in Gulfton expect it to succeed in the current climate. "People have been saying there's no need to count everybody because in the end, even if everybody's counted, those resources are not going to trickle down to the undocumented people," says Juarez. "I'm optimistic they're going to get a better count, because of the resources," he concedes, before adding, "but it's not going to be enough."

Ironically, it may be that the politics of immigration have made places like Gulfton too American for government to do its job, even among census believers like Evelyn DeLeon. "It's important and I hope there is change, but . . ." She stops to gather her thoughts, before settling on a starkly American idea about it all: "Whether the census is supposed to provide this help or not, I'm going to have to do this on my own."

| "The 2010 census will be the first time in the nation's history when a same-sex couple could actually hold a marriage license and thus accurately identify themselves as 'married.'"

The 2010 Census Will Count Same-Sex Married Couples for the First Time

Lisa Keen

In the following viewpoint, Lisa Keen reports that the 2010 census will mark the first opportunity for same-sex married couples to portray themselves as such on the country's official record of the population. Keen further cites individuals within the lesbian, gay bisexual, and transgender (LGBT) community who count the inclusion of same-sex couples in the census as a victory for tolerance and expansion of civil rights for homosexual people. While the change does represent a milestone in the recognition of individuals of the same sex who consider themselves to be in a marriage, many of the states where these couples live do not recognize their unions in legal terms. Keen argues that this discrepancy along with perceived failures of the Barack Obama admin-

istration to uphold promises to expand LGBT rights has led to ongoing anger within this community. Still, the author maintains that this step shows a new interpretation of the Defense of Marriage Act, which is often invoked to ban same-sex marriage, by the Obama administration with regard to the census that differs from that of all previous administrations. Keen is a journalist who has reported on LGBT issues for more than twenty years.

As you read, consider the following questions:

1. In what ways, according to the author, do "numbers count in Washington" both generally and for the LGBT community specifically?

2. What advice did the Human Rights Campaign give to LGBT people with regard to completing the marital status portion of the census form?

3. As cited by the author, how many same-sex couples were wed in California?

It has been widely reported in the last few days [June 2009] that "the White House said" it was going to start counting same-sex married couples in the U.S. census. Although it's hard to pin down just exactly who in the White House said exactly what, the news is apparently true and it's a big deal to many in the LGBT [lesbian, gay, bisexual, and transgender] community. Numbers count in Washington—they justify programs, illustrate the need for certain bills, and give a sense of size for a particular voting bloc. And they can counter a general tendency toward simply ignoring the existence of gays.

"This is a huge win for our community," said Rea Carey, executive director of the National Gay and Lesbian Task Force. "Our community and allies stood up and refused to allow same-sex marriages, our families, and our children to be rendered invisible in the picture of our country provided through the census."

Carey noted the decision to change the census policy toward counting same-sex married couples "gives us hope that we will also be able to get the federal government to include lesbian, gay, bisexual, and transgender people in the data and reporting on other critical issues, including those having to do with our health, economic issues, safety and life circumstances."

Gay Representatives Barney Frank (D-Massachusetts), Tammy Baldwin (D-Wisconsin), and Jared Polis (D-Colorado) issued a joint press release applauding the "announcement" that the "Obama administration is seeking ways to include same-sex marriages, unions, and partnerships in 2010 census data."

Same-Sex Couple Reporting Will No Longer Be Altered

Neither the White House nor the Census Bureau issued a press release about the change, and bureau spokesman Jack Martin noted that it does not affect the questionnaire itself. Among the 14 choices for describing the relationship of "Person 2" to "Person 1" are still "husband or wife" and "unmarried partner."

Martin said the bureau is developing written guidelines now to advise affected citizens how to fill out the form. The Human Rights Campaign has already set up a web page that advises LGBT people who are "living with your married spouse" to check "husband or wife," and other couples to check "unmarried partner."

LGBT population data expert Gary Gates with UCLA's [University of California, Los Angeles] Williams Institute said the change has an impact "only on post-data collection processing." The change in processing will allow same-sex couples who are legally married to identify as each other's "husband or wife."

Prior to 2000, there was no designation that enabled same-sex couples to accurately describe their relationship, and when a same-sex partner checked off the designation of "husband or wife," the census bureau altered the gender of one of the two people, assuming they had accidentally misidentified their gender.

Starting in 2000, the census form provided the new designation of "unmarried partners," which both same-sex couples and unmarried heterosexual couples could choose.

The 2010 census will be the first time in the nation's history when a same-sex couple could actually hold a marriage license and thus accurately identify themselves as "married." Starting in 2004, Massachusetts began issuing licenses to same-sex couples. Now, five additional states do, and New Hampshire will start doing so in January. In California, an estimated 18,000 same-sex couples were married during the five months the state allowed such unions. Those marriages were held to be valid by the state Supreme Court in its decision last month that also upheld Proposition 8, which has since eliminated the right of same-sex couples to wed.

The change in the census "will not explicitly count civil unions and/or domestic partners," said Gates. But, he said, "it is possible" census officials will "begin" consideration of how to change the annual American Community Survey to count civil unions and domestic partners—a "much bigger and more expensive proposition."

Gates also noted that, while the censuses in 1990 and 2000 were politically unpopular with the LGBT community, they were based on "sound scientific reasoning."

"And in 2010," said Gates, "they are again doing the right thing scientifically, which comports with the right thing politically."

"Granted, change at the census can be a bit slow and can require prodding," said Gates, "but they are not the bad guys."

The LGBT community has been discussing and "prodding" for a change in the census since before 1990, and the change for 2010 is another important incremental change.

Census Victory Highlights Other Political Failures

But the news does not appear to have made a dent in the anger that erupted this month over a Justice Department brief concerning same-sex marriage. Pro-gay marriage demonstrators stood outside a Democratic National Committee fundraiser in Boston Tuesday night, where Vice President Joe Biden was the keynote speaker. A growing number of well-known gay Democratic supporters have said they will not attend an LGBT Democratic fund-raiser in Washington, D.C., tonight (Thursday, June 25).

Nor has the census news quelled a growing chorus of activists pressuring President Barack Obama to do more to end the military's anti-gay "Don't Ask, Don't Tell" [DADT] policy [which, until September 20, 2011, prohibited openly gay individuals from serving in the U.S. military]. The Servicemembers Legal Defense Network [SLDN] announced Tuesday that it is organizing a march to the White House on Saturday, June 27, "to urge President Obama to break his continued silence on repealing" that law.

"As long as the president remains silent on DADT repeal," said the SLDN statement, "men and women in the military will continue to be fired at a clip of two per day on average. The sense of urgency is palpable."

And so continues the tug-of-war. The White House is preparing a commemoration of the 40th anniversary of the Stonewall Rebellion [an event that occurred on June 28, 1969, when demonstrations at the Stonewall Inn in Greenwich Village became a riot as members of the gay community in New York City rebelled against institutionalized oppression] to be held in the East Room on Monday, June 29, but news of that leaked out only thanks to a blog of the *New York Times*. The White House withheld information about its plans even after the *Times* published its report online.

"It's hard to have any other impression after reading [the *Times* report] than the Obama administration would really like to hustle the invitees to this Stonewall event through some back door, and hustle the queers back out ASAP," wrote political blogger Pam Spaulding.

The Obama Justice Department agreed to discuss with gay legal advocates the legal challenges against the Defense of Marriage Act [DOMA]. And White House staff secretary and assistant to the president Lisa Brown told an audience attending a conference of the American Constitution Society June 19 that "there's no question" that there were "some cites" in the DOJ [Department of Justice] brief in the *Smelt* case [*Arthur Smelt et al. v. United States et al.*, which sought to have the Defense of Marriage Act declared unconstitutional] "that should not have been in there." Brown qualified her remark, saying it was a "personal statement."

But asked about Brown's remarks at a press briefing Monday, White House press secretary Robert Gibbs appeared to try to deflect the question by noting that "Lisa [Brown] is the staff secretary." (Although the position is an administrative one in some regards, it is also "the last substantive stop," said Brown, before a document is signed by the president. Brown is also a lawyer and a former executive director of the American Constitution Society.)

When a reporter asked him whether any discussion was under way to consider modifying DOJ's position in the marriage lawsuits, Gibbs replied, "Not that I'm aware of."

Gibbs has delivered the "Not that I'm aware of" line or a similar non-response on several occasions when asked about gay-related issues.

New Interpretations of the Defense of Marriage Act

Meanwhile, back on the census, the White House press office alerted this reporter to the decision to count same-sex married couples as married by sending her an e-mail that carried a *Wall Street Journal* article reporting the change. The article stated that "the White House said" on June 18 that "it was seeking ways" to count "same-sex marriages, unions, and partnerships" in the 2010 census. (As mentioned earlier, the change in processing the data will count only same-sex couples who identify as a "husband or wife," not civil unions or domestic partnerships.)

During the [President Bill] Clinton administration, the Census Bureau declared that it could not count same-sex couples who were married as married, contending that the 1996 Defense of Marriage Act prohibited it from doing so. But, the Census Bureau under Obama apparently has a different understanding of how DOMA does—or doesn't—apply to the processing of data.

"[In conducting the census] the government will give the nation's more than
308 million people the opportunity to
define their racial makeup as one race
or more."

Multiple Racial Classifications Allow Americans to Define Themselves

Haya El Nasser

*Changes in recent census forms are allowing respondents to clas-
sify themselves beyond multiracial by permitting them to check
more than one racial category when identifying their race. In the
following viewpoint, Haya El Nasser, a writer for* USA Today,
*reports that many people are pleased with this new opportunity
because they felt confined by the "multi-race" box that appeared
on census documents prior to 2000. According to El Nasser, by
moving beyond a few fixed racial categories, the census is reflecting the greater diversity in America and helping people feel better about how they choose to define themselves. As El Nasser reports, some observers even believe the move will help the nation
become a "post-racial" society in which racial distinctions will
become less and less important.*

As you read, consider the following questions:

1. As El Nasser reports, by what year does the Census Bureau predict there will be no racial or ethnic majority in the United States?

2. What percentage of the US population identifies itself as mixed-race on census surveys, according to the author?

3. As El Nasser writes, how many states had at least a 20 percent increase in mixed-race marriages since 2000?

Jennifer Harvey was raised by her white mother and white stepfather in what she calls "a Caucasian world." Harvey never met her father but she knew he was black and Cuban. That made her Hispanic, white and black.

"Blacks think I'm black," she says. "Hispanics think I'm Hispanic. Honestly, I don't identify with either bucket wholeheartedly—Caucasian, black or Hispanic."

After high school, living on her own in Alabama, she applied for a new driver's license. The state, on its own, identified her as black. "I felt I had been branded something I wasn't," says Harvey, 40, an administrative assistant for a Houston energy company.

Reporting Race on the Census

This month [March 2010], the Census Bureau will remind Americans that racial classifications remain an integral part of the country's social and legal fabric while, at the same time, recognizing that racial lines are blurring for a growing number of people such as Harvey. The government will give the nation's more than 308 million people the opportunity to define their racial makeup as one race or more.

The agency expects the number of people who choose multiple races to be significantly higher than the 2000 census, when the government first allowed more than one race choice. Responses to this year's survey will provide for the first time a glimpse at the evolution of racial identification: Those who were children in 2000 and were identified as one race by their parents may respond differently as adults today and select more than one.

"It's a historic opportunity to see how things have changed or how things have not changed," says Nicholas [A.] Jones, chief of the Census Bureau racial statistics branch. Multiracial Americans are "one of the fastest-growing demographic groups in the country. There's an increasing number of children born to parents of different races."

When Barack Obama was elected the nation's first black president in 2008, some academics and political analysts suggested the watershed event could represent the dawning of a post-racial era in a land that has struggled over race relations for four centuries.

At the same time, growing ethnic and racial diversity fueled by record immigration and rates of interracial marriages have made the USA's demographics far more complex. By 2050, there will be no racial or ethnic majority as the share of non-Hispanic whites slips below 50%, according to Census [Bureau] projections.

"It's showing that tomorrow's children and their children will in fact be multiracial, leading to a potential post-racial society," says William Frey, demographer at the Brookings Institution.

"The issue isn't just multi-race," says census historian Margo Anderson, professor at the University of Wisconsin-Milwaukee. "It's the blurring of the very traditional black vs. white. Categories that held until about 1980 are shifting in large numbers. . . . The clarity is breaking down."

Census Questions in Detail

2010 census forms will arrive in more than 135 million households by the middle of March. Two of the 10 questions on the form will prompt soul-searching for some multiracial people such as Harvey and routine responses from millions of others.

Question No. 8 asks if anyone in the household is Hispanic, Latino or of Spanish origin. That's a question about ethnicity.

Question No. 9 asks the race of every person in the household—regardless of whether they're Hispanic. The instructions specify: "Mark one or more boxes." Choices include white, black, American Indian or Alaska Native, Asian, Native Hawaiian or other Pacific Islander.

It also has one more box: "Some other race." That's the catch-all category that many Hispanics and people who don't see themselves as fitting in existing race categories pick. In the past, it also has lured wags who write in their race as "human," "Vulcan" or "Texan."

Why does the government ask about race and ethnicity?

Federal agencies need the information to monitor compliance with anti-discrimination laws such as the Voting Rights Act and the Civil Rights Act, fair employment practices and affirmative action mandates.

Only 2.3% of the population—about 7 million—identify themselves as being of more than one race, according to recent census surveys. That figure has remained constant since 2000. But mixed-race marriages have jumped 20% since 2000 to 4.5 million, or 8% of the total.

The number of people reporting more than one race may seem small, Frey says, because for generations, there had not been wide social acceptance of mixed-race individuals.

"A lot of people who were part American Indian never said they were part American Indian until it became more popular to do that," Frey says. "It's not in their consciousness as much as it might be in the future."

Jones agrees. "If the trends continue—rising number of interracial relationships and marriages, rising number of births (in) those relationships and increasing awareness of racial identity—we may see an increase" in people listing themselves as multiracial, he says.

For Harvey, the gap between genetic reality and life experiences sent her in search of her "blackness" and on a lifelong struggle with racial identity. Her quest caused a break with her family that has since been patched. She has three daughters now. Their fathers are black.

Harvey likes the chance in this year's census to identify all the races in her heritage but still is not sure what she'll report for her daughters.

"The youngest (4 years old) wants to be identified as black," she says. "I'm still grappling with that. If I can get Hispanic and black for them, that's the ideal."

How People View Themselves

Obama, born to a black father and a white mother, is not only the first black president but the first biracial president.

During his successful campaign in 2008, Obama referred to himself as black but also referred to his roots in Hawaii, where he was raised by his white mother. When the Obamas' census form arrives at 1600 Pennsylvania Ave., will he identify himself as black or as black and white? The White House declines to say.

The census may never truly reflect the actual number of people in the USA who are of more than one race. That's because responses are based on how people view themselves, how they think they are perceived or how they choose to be represented in the national count.

"The issue of perception is central," says Ann Morning, a sociology professor at New York University. In an article titled "Who Is Multiracial?" she estimated that about one-third of the U.S. population has some mixed-racial ancestry going back several generations. She predicts young generations will be more embracing of their multiracial heritage.

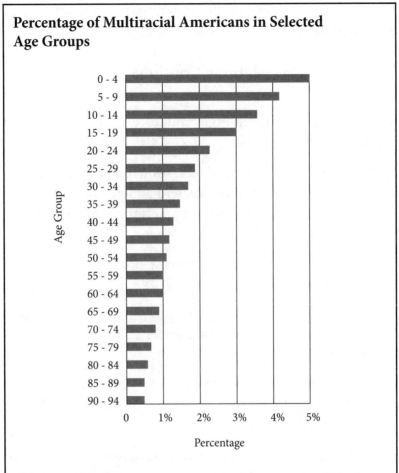

Percentage of Multiracial Americans in Selected Age Groups

TAKEN FROM: 2005-2007 Census Bureau data reported in Haya El Nasser, "Multiracial No Longer Boxed in by the Census," *USA Today*, March 15, 2010. www.usatoday.com.

Morning is African American. But she also has English, Chinese and American Indian ancestry. Since 2000, she has checked off black, white, Asian and American Indian.

"The bigger thing is how I will mark my daughters," Morning says. Their dad is Italian, and she believes most people will look at her daughters as white. For now, she'll check all the boxes for them, too.

"There is a segment of the community that is very proud of having multiple ethnicities or backgrounds," Jones says.

Mixed-Raced Populations Continue to Grow

Racial identity is increasingly muddled as the number of mixed-race unions grows:

- About three of 10 marriages involving Hispanics or Asians are now mixed-race, and almost one of six involving blacks are mixed race, according to an analysis by demographer Frey.

- About 9% of marriages involving non-Hispanic whites are mixed.

- A 10th or more of all marriages in 13 states—most in the West—were mixed race in 2008.

- Thirty-six states had at least a 20% increase in mixed-race marriages since 2000, including Florida, Virginia and Texas. A fifth of marriages in California and New Mexico were mixed.

"For some, the multi-race response option represented an opportunity to acknowledge both parents," says Roderick Harrison, a demographer at Howard University and the Joint Center for Political and Economic Studies in Washington. "But for a lot of others, it's like, 'OK, are you going to turn your back on the rest of us?' . . . A lot of the racial and ethnic politics of the census are that we want the biggest numbers possible for our groups."

The census has a long-lasting effect on politics and money. Population counts every 10 years decide the number of seats every state gets in the U.S. House of Representatives and determine how more than $400 billion a year in federal aid is allocated.

"I know it's valuable information if you're doing economic development or dispensing a certain amount of money to areas that need it," says Stewart Cockburn, 39, who lost his job in textile sales in September. "My point about race in general in this country is that we're just never going to get past it if we keep asking about it."

Cockburn, of Greensboro, N.C., says he's Scottish and Irish and has a great-grandmother who was Cherokee.

"I don't understand why everyone makes such a big deal about race," he says. "Maybe one day we will no longer care about race, ethnicity or the color of another person's skin."

Donna Edwards, of Santa Monica, Calif, says it's important that the federal government allows people to identify more than one race. "It's about time, isn't it?" says Edwards, who is half-Japanese and half-German/Scottish/Welsh and spent years frustrated by forms that boxed her into one or the other.

"That was annoying," says Edwards, 50, a freelance production supervisor of national TV ads. "I would sit there for about a minute and get a little miffed and I would end up picking white. . . . Isn't that reverse discrimination? I could no more say I'm just white than I could say I'm just Japanese."

Surveys suggest that younger generations are much less concerned with race than older Americans, Harrison says.

"For the younger part of our society, race is going to be less of a factor when they decide partners, whom they're going to church with, where they're going to live," Frey says. "It won't be exactly color-blind but much more color-blind."

In this day and age, Edwards says, "with all the travel we can do, we're not all going to be white or black. . . . At some point we're all going to be so mixed, we're all going to be the same color."

> "Despite the federal government's setting
> standards more than a decade ago, data
> on race and ethnicity are being col-
> lected and aggregated in an assortment
> of ways. The lack of uniformity is mak-
> ing comparison and analysis extremely
> difficult across fields and across time."

Multiple Racial Classifications Can Skew Accurate Counts

Susan Saulny

Susan Saulny is a national correspondent at the New York Times.
*In the following viewpoint, she notes that several government
bodies that survey the racial makeup of the United States employ
different methods of defining multiracial respondents. Some only
allow survey respondents to categorize themselves as being of
"two or more races" or simply "other." Other surveys, such as the
US census, have expanded racial categorization, permitting respondents to check off as many racial delineations as they wish.
Saulny reports that the different methods can lead to statistical
problems, especially in instances when data is cross-referenced
between surveys. Even the broadening of racial categorization*

can lead to research errors, Saulny writes, because it is difficult to compare, for example, census statistics from before 2000 (the first year the expanded categorization was implemented) and the new census surveys.

As you read, consider the following questions:

1. According to Saulny, who will be reported as simply "Hispanic" on Department of Education forms and surveys that ask about race?

2. What reasons does Saulny give for why the US Census Bureau recently chose to change its policy and let respondents check as many race boxes as desired?

3. As Saulny reports, why does the National Center for Health Statistics have problems gathering accurate race data from birth certificates?

The federal Department of Education would categorize Michelle López-Mullins—a university student who is of Peruvian, Chinese, Irish, Shawnee and Cherokee descent—as "Hispanic." But the National Center for Health Statistics, the government agency that tracks data on births and deaths, would pronounce her "Asian" and "Hispanic." And what does Ms. López-Mullins's birth certificate from the state of Maryland say? It doesn't mention her race.

Ms. López-Mullins, 20, usually marks "other" on surveys these days, but when she filled out a census form last year, she chose Asian, Hispanic, Native American and white.

The chameleon-like quality of Ms. López-Mullins's racial and ethnic identification might seem trivial except that statistics on ethnicity and race are used for many important purposes. These include assessing disparities in health, education, employment and housing, enforcing civil rights protections, and deciding who might qualify for special consideration as members of underrepresented minority groups.

But when it comes to keeping racial statistics, the nation is in transition, moving, often without uniformity, from the old "mark one box" limit to allowing citizens to check as many boxes as their backgrounds demand. Changes in how Americans are counted by race and ethnicity are meant to improve the precision with which the nation's growing diversity is gauged: the number of mixed-race Americans, for example, is rising rapidly, largely because of increases in immigration and intermarriage in the past two decades. (One in seven new marriages is now interracial or interethnic.)

Many Data Collection Methods Can Lead to Imprecision

In the process, however, a measurement problem has emerged. Despite the federal government's setting standards more than a decade ago, data on race and ethnicity are being collected and aggregated in an assortment of ways. The lack of uniformity is making comparison and analysis extremely difficult across fields and across time.

Under Department of Education requirements that take effect this year, for instance, any student like Ms. López-Mullins who acknowledges even partial Hispanic ethnicity will, regardless of race, be reported to federal officials only as Hispanic. And students of non-Hispanic mixed parentage who choose more than one race will be placed in a "two or more races" category, a catchall that detractors describe as inadequately detailed. A child of black and American Indian parents, for example, would be in the same category as, say, a child of white and Asian parents.

The new standards for kindergarten through 12th grades and higher education will probably increase the nationwide student population of Hispanics, and could erase some "black" students who will now be counted as Hispanic or as multiracial (in the "two or more races category"). And reclassifying large numbers of white Hispanic students as simply Hispanic has the potential to mask the difference between minority and white students' test scores, grades and graduation rates—the so-called achievement gap, a target of federal reform efforts that has plagued schools for decades.

"They're all lumped together—blacks, Asians and Latinos—and they all look the same from the data perspective," said Daniel J. Losen, a policy expert for the Civil Rights Project at the University of California, Los Angeles, referring to the Department of Education aggregation. "But the reality is much different. There are different kinds of discrimination experienced by these subgroups."

"It's a big problem for researchers," Mr. Losen continued, "because it throws a monkey wrench in our efforts at accountability, student tracking and the study of trends."

Education officials say the changes will more accurately reflect how Americans see themselves. The standards were also devised to save schools time and money. If schools were to report on every possible racial and ethnic combination to the federal authorities, there would be dozens of possibilities. It is simply easier to call students "two or more races."

"Ultimately, the department's final requirements aim to strike the balance," said Russlynn H. Ali, the department's assistant secretary for civil rights, "between minimizing the burden for local education agencies while also ensuring the availability of high-quality racial and ethnic data."

A Call for More Transparency

But critics, including elected officials and the Citizens' Commission on Civil Rights, a Washington group that monitors federal policy and practices, have called the move disturbing and want more transparency. While the policy was still in developmental stages, the commission urged the Department of Education to "evaluate alternative approaches, including those adopted by the U.S. Census" to track students' race.

In 2006, 62 members of Congress signed a letter to the education secretary at the time, Margaret Spellings, expressing "utmost concern" about the changes. And research by the Harvard Civil Rights Project in 2006 showed that the new method of race reporting would result in a significant reduction in the black student population nationally, producing data that it called "questionable and often meaningless."

That could affect responsibilities held by the Department of Education in areas including civil rights enforcement, program monitoring, and the identification and placement of students in special education. The numbers also affect areas like research and statistical analysis, and school and teacher accountability when it comes to student achievement and academic progress.

"We believe that these changes are not supported by good research," the Harvard report stated.

In the late 1990s, the Census Bureau abandoned the idea of a catchall "multiracial" classification in favor of letting people check more than one box, in part because many Americans did not understand what multiracial meant. And a federal task force had concluded that creating a multiracial category would "add to racial tensions and further fragmentation" of the population.

The N.A.A.C.P. [National Association for the Advancement of Colored People] had vowed "vigorous resistance" to the notion of a multiracial catchall, concerned that such an option would diminish minority numbers, particularly blacks, in government counts.

But Project RACE, for Reclassify All Children Equally, one of the largest and most vocal multiracial advocacy groups, and its president, Susan Graham, a white mother of biracial children, were among those who had pushed equally hard for a multiracial classification.

"It is simply ridiculous that multiracial children should have to have the sanction and approval of other minority groups in order to have their own identity," Ms. Graham testified before Congress in 1997.

Changes in Census Race Categories Are Still Problematic

The Census Bureau's solution may have added layers of complexity for demographers—creating 63 categories of possible racial combinations—but it laid to rest fears from civil rights advocates that adding a multiracial category would diminish the number of blacks, Asians or American Indians in official government counts, since multiracial people are counted in the ranks of all of the races they check. (This does not distort the total population of the United States because that number is based on how many people answer the census questionnaire, not on adding the totals from each racial column.)

Even the Census Bureau acknowledges that accurately counting the multiracial population is a challenge and says it continues to explore ways to do it better, said Nicholas A. Jones, chief of the racial statistics branch. Some people of mixed race were fickle about their racial identifications in early tests of the new, more expansive methods, changing their answers from interview to interview.

Moreover, because the census in 2000 began allowing respondents to mark as many races as they wanted, today's numbers are not directly comparable with those before 2000.

The National Center for Health Statistics collects vital statistics from the states to document the health of the population. When it comes to collecting birth certificate information, though, the center encounters a problem: 38 states and the District of Columbia report race data in the new and more expansive manner that allows for the recording of more than one race. But a dozen states do not, because they still use old

Percentage of State Population of Mixed Race, 2010

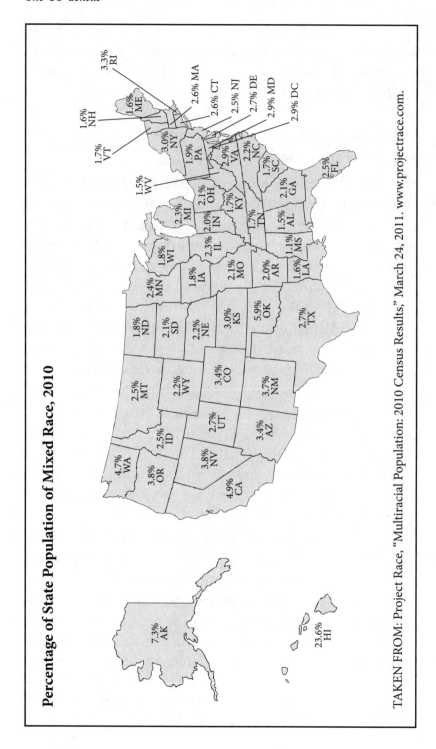

TAKEN FROM: Project Race, "Multiracial Population: 2010 Census Results," March 24, 2011. www.projectrace.com.

data systems and outdated forms. As a result, the center cannot produce consistent national data for what it calls "medical and health purposes only."

To get around that problem, the center reclassifies mixed-race births using a complex algorithm. For example, a birth to a parent who marked white, Asian and Native American would be declared just one of those races, depending on a number of variables in a probability model, like sex, age of the mother and place of birth. (Birth data is reported, in most cases, by the race of the mother.)

States were supposed to begin moving to the new way of collecting data in 2003, but a lack of resources has proved a hurdle for many and forced the center for health statistics to come up with this solution, which officials call temporary.

"There are over four million births every year, so we can't possibly get back to the mother and see which race she would prefer," said Stephanie Ventura, chief of the reproductive statistics branch at the center. "We don't do that on birth or death certificates."

Personal Choice vs. the Demands of Data Collectors

Speaking of the complexities of keeping track of people by race now that the multiracial population is growing, Jeffrey S. Passel, a senior demographer at the Pew Hispanic Center, said, "The issue is multiplied manifold if you start thinking about HR [Human Resources] departments and private firms."

The Equal Employment Opportunity Commission [E.E.O.C.] mandates that most companies provide an annual count of their workers by race, ethnicity and gender. (The E.E.O.C. strongly suggests that companies ask workers how they identity themselves, as opposed to making assumptions based on appearance.) In 2007, the E.E.O.C. added a "two or more races" category.

Today, federal education officials defend their changes as an improvement over the more limited choices of the past, when students were identified by only one race and Hispanics were often undercounted. They also say they are merely trying to abide by orders from the Office of Management and Budget—which sets standards on how federal agencies keep statistics—that all agencies try to collect data in a two-part question: the first focused on Hispanic ethnicity and the second on race, allowing the reporting of more than one.

"The department strongly believes that the new requirements will help educators and others better serve students who identify with more than one race and Hispanic/Latino students, which is the fastest growing population in our schools today," said Ms. Ali, the assistant education secretary. Further, she said, schools are required to retain the original, more detailed answers to racial survey questions that they collect but do not report to the federal authorities—in case discrimination complaints arise, for instance.

"If our goal is to gather better information," said Louie Gong, a former president of Mavin [Foundation], a mixed-race advocacy group based in Seattle, "then you'd think we wouldn't begin by arbitrarily reallocating people to categories they didn't pick."

Many mixed-race Americans are wary of statistics on race. In a typical year, Ms. López-Mullins, the Peruvian-Chinese-Irish-Shawnee-Cherokee president of a multiracial student group at the University of Maryland, says she is asked to fill out forms for school, for extracurricular activities and standardized tests, for example, that follow no set standards in asking the questions or gathering the answers.

"It's always, 'How can these multiracial individuals best benefit us? What category can we put them in to fulfill something?'" she said. "I figure there's such a large margin of error with that kind of ridiculous accounting anyway, I'm totally against it."

For years, when asked her race, she checked everything that applied: Hispanic, Asian, white and Native American. And if she is now confronted with a blank space for her race, she might challenge the form with a question of her own: "What does this tell you?"

The Department of Education says that answer tells a lot, and that its new race reporting standards are a step forward, particularly since the department will get a more accurate count of Hispanics, the nation's largest minority.

"Balancing these goals is difficult," Ms. Ali said, "particularly in light of how personal this issue is for many people."

"*Nonprofit leaders hope their organizations can serve as 'trusted voices' in neighborhoods dominated by people who are likely to be left out.*"

Grant Makers Commit Millions to Help Ensure Accurate Census

Marty Michaels

Marty Michaels is a former editor of the Chronicle of Philanthropy. *In the following viewpoint, Michaels insists that charitable foundations have a great influence on the 2010 census. She maintains that philanthropic groups are waging their own campaigns to alert people—especially undercounted immigrants and other minorities—about the importance of being counted in the census. Spending millions of dollars, these organizations are hoping to encourage more underrepresented residents to fill out their census forms to earn more federal monetary support for their communities. Michaels also notes that many charitable campaigns are aimed at allaying fears of immigrants who might assume their census information could be used against them.*

Marty Michaels, "Grant Makers Commit Millions to Help Ensure Accurate Census," Chronicle of Philanthropy, vol. 22, no. 7, February 25, 2010. pp. 1–22. Copyright © 2010 by the Chronicle of Philanthropy.

As you read, consider the following questions:

1. According to Michaels, what natural and man-made catastrophes have made census taking a problem for some communities?

2. As the author reports, about how many people did the Census Bureau estimate it undercounted (or missed) during the 2000 census?

3. As Michaels explains, what percentage of a community must be Latino for the Census Bureau to offer census documents in English and Spanish in 2010?

*A*t stake in the tally: More than $4-trillion in money governments apportion to the people charities serve.

As the 2010 census nears its official start in March, nonprofit leaders are raising serious concerns about the government's ability to achieve an accurate tally in this once-a-decade population count.

In response, foundations have poured tens of millions of dollars into nonprofit census efforts, but many nonprofit leaders say much more is needed.

The stakes are enormous: The data will be used not only to apportion House seats and reshape congressional districts but also to parcel out more than $400 billion each year in federal funds—some $4 trillion over the next decade for education, health care, and other critical social services. The national per-person average for annual federal funds allocated on the basis of census data is now $1,415, according to the Brookings Institution—that is, every person counted will "bring in" $14,150 over the next decade. And those figures don't even take into account the billions of dollars that flow from state and local apportionments based on census data.

By the same token, schools, inner-city health clinics, literacy and job-training programs, and other crucial social service providers stand to lose that money in an undercount.

Yet charity observers say that what was already an unwieldy process has worsened with the recession, the home-foreclosure crisis, and Hurricanes Katrina and Rita. Hundreds of thousands of people have been forced from their homes and apartments into temporary quarters, making it difficult for census workers to reach them.

Another issue at play is what the Naleo Educational Fund, a Los Angeles Latino-rights group, calls "the increasingly xenophobic environment surrounding the immigration debate."

"The population is more diverse, speaking more languages, and we are in an environment that's less hospitable to immigrants, who are already difficult to count," says Terri Ann Lowenthal, a consultant in Stamford, Conn., who works with nonprofit and other groups on census-related issues. "Plus, this is the first post-9/11 census, and people are more concerned about their privacy and sharing information."

Nonprofit leaders hope their organizations can serve as "trusted voices" in neighborhoods dominated by people who are likely to be left out, helping convince them that it is safe and important to participate in the census.

"Make no mistake—the census is the preeminent civil rights issue of 2010," says Wade Henderson, president of the Leadership Conference Education Fund, in Washington.

His organization is running ads in English, Chinese, and Spanish on 1,500 buses as part of an eight-city campaign to encourage people to fill out their census forms.

Nonprofit Support

While precise figures are hard to come by, the Census Bureau estimates that the 2000 census undercounted—or "missed"—at least 6.4 million people, the overwhelming majority of them minorities, poor people, and children.

In response, nonprofit efforts are stressing activities designed to reach the nation's growing Hispanic population, re-

Influencing a Higher Response

Nonprofits are encouraged to partner with the census to help reach out to hard-to-count populations.... Nonprofits are vital to this process because of the trust already established within the community and because it's been shown that similar cultural backgrounds influence a higher response.

Amanda Stitt,
"A Primer on the Census: Counting Heads and Counting Costs,"
Progressive Women's Alliance, February 17, 2010.
www.progressivewomensalliance.org.

cent immigrants, African-Americans, low-income renters, homeless people, and other types of people who have historically been undercounted.

To help persuade Americans to participate, the U.S. Census Bureau began a $133-million multimedia advertising blitz in mid-January.

Yet charity leaders say that local service and civil rights groups have a distinct advantage in motivating hard-to-count people to participate.

At least one national network has formed to promote such work—the Funders Census Initiative, an ad hoc group that advocates greater involvement in the 2010 census among grant makers and their grantees.

Members include the Ford Foundation, which has allocated $11 million since summer 2008 to 26 grantees and is considering giving another $4 million to some 17 groups, and the Open Society Institute, which gave slightly more than $1 million in 2009 for direct census activities and has also increased general-support awards to current grantees that work to encourage people to participate in the upcoming census.

To date, the Funders Census Initiative's activities have included helping grant makers draft requests for proposals and assess grant applications and providing grantees with census materials and assistance in navigating the Census Bureau's bureaucracy.

Nonprofit leaders hope to drum up additional philanthropic dollars in the coming months.

"There are so many foundations supporting activities like health care for the poor and affordable housing and community development," says Ms. Lowenthal. "Well, there are billions of dollars in federal funds and billions more in state funds that are allocated to local groups using census data."

Adds Bridgette Rongitsch, national director of the Nonprofit Voter Engagement Network, in St. Paul, "Even if you're having to stretch your resources some, the dividends will far outweigh that extra effort. We certainly don't want any money left on the table."

Ms. Rongitsch's group has held free monthly Webinars since July that show nonprofit organizations how to integrate census-related activities into their other activities.

The events have "maxed out" at up to 200 participants, she says, and the presentation is now available for download on the group's Web site.

The network is also planning state-specific Webinars, and in January unveiled new materials for groups that work on homelessness, immigration, criminal justice, and other relevant issues.

Tough Cases

Reaching people from a diverse range of ethnic backgrounds remains a key challenge.

The Asian American Legal Defense and Education Fund, a New York advocacy group, unveiled its Twenty10 Project in

August, beginning with the release of census-education materials in English and 13 other languages, including Arabic, Khmer, Urdu, and Vietnamese.

The fact sheets provide basic information about the importance of participating in the census, including language-assistance options.

Glenn D. Magpantay, a staff lawyer and director of the project, says the organization also has been contacting regional census officials to ensure that the hiring of census-outreach staff members adequately reflects the ethnic composition of the neighborhoods where they will work.

The fund's largest census-related effort will focus on confidentiality. "We need to be sure that the census protects the anonymity of undocumented immigrants," says Mr. Magpantay.

Officials at the Naleo Educational Fund voice similar concerns. Arturo Vargas, the executive director, says that while Hispanics now constitute the second-largest ethnic group in the United States, they are increasingly dispersed around the country rather than concentrated only in California, Texas, and a few other regions as in the past.

And in these new locales, says Mr. Vargas, Hispanics may shy away from anything government related if they don't have accurate information on confidentiality and civil rights issues.

To counter this, his group's census-education campaign—dubbed Ya Es Hora! Hágase Contar! (It's Time! Make Yourself Count!)—includes a focus on geographic pockets in Georgia, North Carolina, and elsewhere in the South that have growing numbers of Hispanic residents.

To convey its message, Naleo is relying primarily on a network of small, local groups nationwide and on Entravision, impreMedia, and Univision, the country's three predominant Spanish-language media enterprises, which are running both television and radio ads.

But the effort is still fraught with problems, says Mr. Vargas. While the Census Bureau will mail out bilingual questionnaires for the first time—"something Latino groups have been asking for for 40 years"—they will be sent out only in areas where the bureau estimates Hispanics make up 20 percent of the population.

Mr. Vargas anticipates communication problems in those areas where many Latinos now live but where they don't reach the 20-percent threshold.

In these new pockets, he adds, there are often no local groups that serve Latinos. "They don't yet have an infrastructure," says Mr. Vargas, "and there are no trusted messengers."

"*As they prepare for this spring's national count, census officials are determined to leave no niche behind.*"

Census Bureau Partnerships with Undercounted Groups Have Helped Boost Participation

Carol Morello

In the following viewpoint, Carol Morello, a staff writer for the Washington Post, *reports on the outreach campaign the US Census Bureau is undertaking to connect with diverse communities across the country. According to Morello, various ethnic, labor, student, and other organizations are helping the bureau reach often hard-to-count populations, spreading the word that census counts benefit communities by attracting federal aid. As Morello writes, more and more undercounted populations are getting the message and participating in greater numbers than in previous census years.*

As you read, consider the following questions:

1. How much money did the US government spend on its 2010 census campaign, as Morello reports?

Carol Morello, "Census Counts on Partnerships to Find Hard-to-Reach Groups," *Washington Post*, January 3, 2010, p. C1.

2. According to Morello, what percentage of District of Columbia residents are considered hard to count?

3. According to the author, how many groups in Washington, D.C., have partnered with the Census Bureau to promote the 2010 census?

George Duangmanee is a financial adviser in the District [of Columbia], an immigrant and an officer in a scholarship program for Asian tennis players. It is the latter role that has made him a catch for the Census Bureau.

Although he did not bother to mail back his questionnaire for the 2000 census, he has been sending e-mails touting the 2010 count to 15,000 people involved in the Thai Tennis Organization. He has enlisted other Thai organizations to help translate census posters into the Thai language and promote the tally at thaicensus.org. He is also passing out water bottles labeled with the 2010 census logo at Asian festivals in the Washington region.

"At first, I had no idea what the census is," said Duangmanee, 38, who was recruited by a census employee hired to approach leaders in communities that are considered hard to count. "Nobody had ever explained to us how important it is. I tell people, if you have a kid who goes to school here, it's important to be counted. Now they understand."

Looking for Undercounted Groups

As they prepare for this spring's national count, census officials are determined to leave no niche behind.

Locally, for example, recruiters have landed representatives of a gay basketball team, immigrants from a chiefdom in Sierra Leone and a Chinese acupuncturist. They have appealed to liquor stores and hardware stores, pizzerias and patisseries, the Nationals and the Mystics [sports teams], Shakespearean scholars, the Woodrow Wilson House and even the CIA [Central Intelligence Agency], asking each to display posters or a stack of brochures.

"My sense was they were talking to everyone, no matter how remote the connection to the census," said Gail Kern Paster, director of the Folger Shakespeare Library, where visitors can pick up a census flier.

This is not the first time the Census Bureau has reached out to groups considered hard to count: the poor, minorities and recent immigrants. But for 2010, the bureau has 3,000 employees, five times as many as 10 years ago, assigned to find "partners" to champion census participation. They have formed alliances with 136,000 groups, houses of worship and businesses. States, counties and municipalities eager to secure a share of almost $480 billion in federal funds allotted on census statistics are linking up with thousands more.

"We're becoming even more diverse than we were 10 years ago," said Wayne Hatcher, director of the regional census office in Charlotte, which is responsible for five states, including Virginia. "I have to make a more concerted effort to find bilingual people and break down the barriers with a new immigrant population that might not understand the census, that might even be afraid of the census."

Community Organizing

For most of the United States, the count will begin April 1. But there will be a symbolic kickoff in late January when Census Bureau Director Robert Groves travels to the Alaskan Inupiat village of Noorvik to count the approximately 600 residents. This week [early January 2010], the bureau will launch 13 vans and recreational vehicles on a road tour, stopping at parades, festivals and the Super Bowl to promote the census. It also will unveil a $300 million advertising campaign this month, momentarily making it one of the biggest advertisers in the country. And it is preparing to hire 1.2 million people for temporary jobs that pay $10 to $25 an hour, mostly to knock on doors in spring and summer and follow up with people who do not mail in their forms.

In the censuses of 1990 and 2000, two of three people responded to the initial mailing. Urban areas, in particular, have many residents who do not respond without prodding. In the District, for example, 55 percent of the residents are considered hard to count. In the 2000 census, the area with the lowest response rate of 45 percent was the heavily African American Ward 8, east of the river, while 77 percent responded in affluent Ward 3, in upper Northwest. That dynamic is replicated across the country. Hoping to boost participation, the city has compiled a list of almost 400 groups that have agreed to promote the census.

Many people need little convincing of the importance of the census for their communities.

"It's a passion of mine," said Juanita Britton, who 10 years ago worked as a marketer for the Census Bureau and now runs the Anacostia Art Gallery and Boutique in Southeast. "As a community organizer, I know the value of the census. I'm in an at-risk community. It's important to educate people that if we're not counted, the money doesn't come in."

Britton has a sign near the cash register inviting her customers to "Ask us about the census." She passes out trinkets such as key chains and squeeze balls that have the census logo.

The Serbian Unity Congress was eager to do its share, if only to get a better handle on how many Serbs are in the United States. Many Serbs who fled the former Yugoslavia when it was a Communist satellite of the Soviet Union were reluctant to cooperate with the government-run census, said Ivana Cerovic, a program director with the group. About 200,000 Serbs were counted in the 2000 census; the organization said it thinks there are closer to 1 million.

Today, it has a message about the census on its website. It has printed bilingual brochures with instructions on filling

out the questionnaire for distribution in 140 Serbian Ortho-
dox churches across the United States.

"This is something we've wanted to do for a long time,"
said Cerovic, who called the Census Bureau and offered to
help.

Campaigns and Trinkets
Make People Aware

More typically, though, census officials have reached out to
groups that have never been approached.

This summer, a census partnership specialist attended the
first national conference of the National Queer Asian Pacific
Islander Alliance, said Ben de Guzman, a Washington-based
program director in the group. The group is distributing census brochures in several Asian languages.

"To the Census Bureau's credit, they have been committed
to reach out to as diverse a constituency as possible," he said.
"Ten years ago, there was no outreach at all to the LGBT [les-
bian, gay, bisexual and transgender] community."

Mohamed Bangura was drawn into census promotion
when he met a bureau employee at an event at the embassy of
Sierra Leone. Bangura, who heads the Koya Progressive Association, a philanthropy made up primarily of people from the
Koya chiefdom in northern Sierra Leone, said he and other
groups intend to lease a hall in March to urge immigrants to
be counted.

"We're really trying to motivate people," said Bangura, a
science teacher in the District. "We educate them that it's important to participate because otherwise, your area may be
underfunded."

Census officials, who spend as much as $3,000 to supply
each group with trinkets and banners, are pleased with the
program.

"When the ad campaign starts in January, that will be the
last push to get on board and start talking about the census,"

said Fernando Armstrong, regional census director in Philadelphia, which covers Maryland and the District. "In reality, anyone can be a good ambassador, talking about the census at the grocery store or in church."

Periodical Bibliography

The following articles have been selected to supplement the diverse views presented in this chapter.

Conor Dougherty   "Population Leaves Heartland Behind," *Wall Street Journal*, April 11, 2011.

John H. Fund   "Making Every Census Count," *American Spectator*, April 2009.

Constance Holden   "America's Uncounted Millions," *Science*, May 22, 2009.

Nathaniel Persily   "The Law of the Census: How to Count, What to Count, Whom to Count, and Where to Count Them," *Cardozo Law Review*, vol. 32, no. 3, 2011.

Raul A. Reyes   "The 2010 Census and Latinos: What Race Are We?," *Christian Science Monitor*, April 6, 2010.

Tim Sullivan   "No Change in How Census Counts Inmates," *Planning*, May 2006.

Anthony Thompson   "Democracy Behind Bars," *New York Times*, August 5, 2009.

Cynthia G. Wagner   "Homosexuality and Family Formation," *Futurist*, May/June 2010.

CHAPTER 3

How Should the US Census Be Reformed?

Chapter Preface

In 2006, the Harris Corporation—a Florida-based international communications and information technology company—received a $595 million contract to develop handheld computers to assist census takers in their door-to-door samplings. Two years later, the project folded due to difficulty of use, soaring costs, and accuracy problems. Peter Orszag, former director of the Office of Management and Budget, decried this failed expenditure. In a June 8, 2010, speech at the Center for American Progress, Orszag stated, "Clearly, we have massive room for improvement. Pursuing that improvement and closing the IT [information technology] gap will help us create a government that is more efficient and less wasteful." Despite Orszag's plea for fiscal austerity, the 2010 census cost $14 billion to administer, and census takers were still using pad and pencil.

Some observers, however, are optimistic about the future marriage of the census and technology. Patrick Thibodeau from ComputerWorld reports that the Census Bureau continues to make reforms in information technology management, including the consolidation of "two major data centers into one, and reducing 52 storage systems to seven," according to an April 13, 2011, commentary. Thibodeau also reports that the Census Bureau will be creating a center for applied technology to bring together its technical staff to devise and coordinate potential cost-saving technologies. The results will eventually yield higher efficiency and lower costs, the bureau anticipates. In addition, the website of the US Census Bureau now runs faster and can handle more users than ever before, thanks to improvements recently instituted.

What kinds of technological solutions the US Census Bureau should adopt is up for debate; however, John D. Sutter from CNN offers a couple of suggestions. In his February 4,

2011, article "Bringing the Census into the Internet Age," he claims that the Bureau ought to collect data via the Internet instead of relying on citizens to send in forms. Sutter refers to Canada's adoption of this method in 2006 as a successful precedent. Follow-through is another challenge for the census. When someone does not submit a form, a person from the bureau will appear at that citizen's doorstep to obtain information. Despite the failed experiment with the handheld devices developed by the Harris Corporation, Sutter suggests moving toward that direction anyway, as Brazil has done since 2006. In Sutter's opinion, the changes the United States ought to consider should reflect Brazil's adoption of new software on smartphones instead of the creation of new, unfamiliar hardware. Census takers already recognize that these technologies can only expedite their process of data collection.

While the adoption of technology appears inevitable for the future of the US census, the authors in the following chapter offer additional avenues for improvement. These controversial areas include what data should be collected, how it should be collected, and who should be eligible for inclusion in census counts.

| *"To choose the [census] raw count is to be wrong on purpose in order to avoid being wrong by accident."*

The Census Will Be Wrong. We Could Fix It.

Jordan Ellenberg

As with previous decennial censuses, the 2010 national count of American citizens again raised questions regarding the accuracy of the count and what could be done to improve it, as in previous years, statistical sampling was debated as a possible method to better determine the number of people living in the country. Using statistical sampling would require the Census Bureau to estimate the number and demographics of people living in given areas by counting a selection of the population and then using mathematical formulas to estimate the total number of people in that location. While many have decried this method as faulty, Jordan Ellenberg argues in the following viewpoint that statistical sampling provides the best opportunity for the Census Bureau to obtain an accurate count of people living in the United States. He maintains that statistical sampling is a complex science developed over decades alongside intensive scientific research that should be recognized as a valid form of enumeration.

Jordan Ellenberg, "The Census Will Be Wrong. We Could Fix It," *Washington Post*, May 1, 2010.

Further, he contends that the census count presents as much of an estimate as statistical sampling, but that currently employed methods are much cruder and prone to error. Ellenberg is an associate professor of mathematics at the University of Wisconsin-Madison.

As you read, consider the following questions:

1. As stated by Ellenberg, how many people were counted twice in the 2000 census?

2. To what other scientific tool does Ellenberg compare statistical sampling?

3. What other circumstances utilize statistical sampling with little resistance, according to the author?

Starting today, thousands of census workers will scour the country, town by town and block by block, trying to identify which addresses have residents and how many they have. The workers' goal: to combine these numbers into a precise reckoning of the American population. As always, they will fail.

They'll get close, sure. But by the Census Bureau's best estimate, the 2000 census counted more than 5 million people twice and millions more not at all. Such errors crop up in every census, demonstrated visibly in 1940, when nearly a half-million more men registered for the draft than officially existed. And those errors aren't demographically uniform; the bureau estimated that the 2000 census undercounted the black population by about 600,000 while bumping up the number of whites by more than 2 million.

How did it know? Because it used a method called statistical sampling to assess the accuracy of its findings, recounting a small selection of addresses after the fact and checking how well the two enumerations agreed. For decades, statisticians inside and outside the census have lobbied with no success to adjust official counts to reflect the information gleaned from statistical sampling. The bureau is stuck in the position of being required to check its work but forbidden to correct it.

Census adjustment has long been a political flash point because the census has winners and losers; an undercount in New York and Chicago could mean fewer members of Congress from blue cities and more from red exurbs. But resistance to adjustment is only partially driven by political interest. It also represents a worrisome mathematical Luddism; adjustment opponents depict statistical estimates as hunches dressed up in fancy mathematical clothes or even plots designed to hijack the census for political ends.

Among the opponents is Sen. Judd Gregg (R-N.H.), who withdrew as the Obama administration's nominee to be commerce secretary in part because of disagreements over the census. Gregg's take on adjustment: "You take guesses based on what you think is the best political outcomes that you want, rather than counting people who actually exist."

But statistical adjustment is not a guess. It's a measurement of something that can't be directly observed, which deserves the same status as the data obtained from any other advanced scientific instrument. The images from an electron microscope may be blurry, and mediated through complex mathematics the layperson can't understand, but they're not guesses. They're facts.

The skepticism that people like Gregg apply to statistics, if applied to other sciences, would get them lumped with the anti-vaccinationists and the homeopaths. The difference? Everyone knows that physics, chemistry and biology have changed radically in the past hundred years; the tools available are fantastically more powerful and reliable than those of the past. Math, by contrast, is taught as if Isaac Newton supplied the final word on the subject.

But survey techniques of the kind the Census Bureau uses didn't exist before the 20th century, and only recently have they been refined enough to improve the accuracy of the census. Justice Clarence Thomas, in a 2002 opinion on sampling, asked: If the Founders had meant the Census Bureau to use statistical sampling technology to improve its count, wouldn't math whiz Thomas Jefferson have used it in the first census? The question is nonsensical. Jefferson could no more have done so than he could have surveyed the population from space.

Note, too, that resistance to statistics is selective. You seldom hear calls for the abolition of data on the gross national product or the unemployment rate, though both are derived from statistical samples. Many who balk at using adjustment to ensure equal representation in Congress are comfortable relying on statistical arguments about DNA when it comes to capital punishment.

Opponents say that statistical adjustment would violate the constitutional requirement of an "actual enumeration" of the population. Justice Antonin Scalia wrote in 1998 that the Constitution's language was "arguably incompatible . . . with gross statistical estimates." The sampling adjustment is indeed an estimate of the population—but so is the unadjusted number, which estimates that the number of Americans missed is zero! To choose the raw count is to be wrong on purpose in order to avoid being wrong by accident.

In any event, the current system is anything but a plain count of heads. Since 1970, a mail-in survey has provided the majority of census data, so what we enumerate is not people but numbers written on a form, which are as likely to be fictional as any statistical estimate. Houses that don't return a form are visited by census workers, but when workers are unable to determine the number of occupants at an address, the census uses statistical properties of the surrounding area to make its best estimate of the ungatherable data. The Supreme Court explicitly upheld this process, called "imputation,"

Using Sampling to Correct the Undercount

Although the Constitution mandates reliance on census data to reapportion the House and, more recently, states' use of that data to draw district lines, claims of inaccuracy have dogged the census since its inception. Since 1940, when comparisons between the April census enumeration and the October Selective Service registration revealed that the census had underreported almost three percent of the male, draft-age population, the Census Bureau has used such techniques as demographic analysis and post-enumeration surveying to estimate the actual undercount rate. . . .

According to the theory on which sampling rests, quantifying the undercount is the main step toward correcting for it. Determining the magnitude of the undercount for various subgroups (or "strata") of the population—broken out by such classifications as age, home ownership, race, or sex—permits the adjustment of the actual counts within each such stratum. In order to determine the degree of undercount in the 2000 census, the Census Bureau planned to take a second, more intensive survey of a demographically selected subset of the population and compare the results of that survey to the actual census. The degree of matchup, that is, the number of people within each "poststratum" who were counted by both the regular and the follow-up surveys, would have served as the predictor for the accuracy of the count for that poststratum. That figure in turn would have served as the basis for the statistical adjustment of the results of the headcount.

"Race, Rights, and Remedies: Census Sampling and the Voting Rights Act," Harvard Law Review, *vol. 114, no. 8, June 2001.*

against a 2002 legal challenge. (The constitutionality of adjustment by sampling has never been directly addressed by the court.)

There are some good reasons to be cautious about sampling adjustment. One could argue that the complex methodology would leave the census vulnerable to politically motivated tampering—though it seems just as likely that, like any mechanism of double-check, adjustment would serve as a brake on tampering. But any such argument has to explain why the government isn't making its best attempt, using available technology, to meet the Constitution's plain demand that we count "the whole number" of Americans—not just the ones who are easy to find. Instead, we've contented ourselves with an enumeration we know not to be actual. We shouldn't be asking the court whether it's constitutional to adjust the census; we should be asking whether it's constitutional not to.

| "You might not get counted, yet your
tax dollars could be spent to count millions of fictitious people."

Statistical Sampling Could Skew Census Counts

Ernest Istook

With undercounts on the decennial census an ongoing concern, some have advocated for the use of statistical sampling—using a small group of people to estimate the larger population—to obtain an accurate count. However, others oppose this method, and in the following viewpoint, Ernest Istook argues that statistical sampling could lead those in power to intentionally skew the count for political gain. While Istook concedes that the Supreme Court has not issued a ruling declaring statistical sampling unconstitutional, he maintains that allowing this technique to be used to enumerate the citizens of the country could result in a count that is not only wrong, but also biased to serve the interests of those in power. The author outlines his concern with the Barack Obama administration's preparations for the 2010 census and concludes that statistical sampling would increase the power of those who conduct the count, creating the potential for a de-

Ernest Istook, "Could 2010 Census Include Make-Believe People?," Heritage Foundation: The Foundry, May 13, 2009. www.heritage.org. Copyright © 2009 by The Heritage Foundation. All rights reserved. Reproduced with permission.

liberate misrepresentation of the population. Istook served as a congressman from Oklahoma for fourteen years and is currently a distinguished fellow at the conservative public policy organization the Heritage Foundation.

As you read, consider the following questions:

1. How many seats in the US House of Representatives does Istook believe could be shifted as a result of statistical sampling on the census?

2. According to Istook, on what sides of the statistical sampling issue do Democrats and Republicans fall?

3. As stated by the author, what did the Supreme Court's 1999 ruling on statistical sampling declare?

L eft-leaning groups want to include millions of pretend people in the real-life 2010 census. It almost happened in 2000. This time, they might get their way.

The administration claims it has "no plans" to use statistical sampling to augment the actual head count next year by adding millions of fictitious people.

The High Stakes of Statistical Sampling

Statistical sampling creates profiles of make-believe people, assigning them an address, a gender, race, age, income, and other characteristics. And it counts them, just as though they were counted by a census worker.

Obama's choice as new census director is University of Michigan Professor Robert Groves, who faces a Senate confirmation hearing May 12 [2009]. Groves is a champion of statistical sampling.

As reported by the Associated Press, "When he was the bureau's associate director, Groves recommended that the 1990 census be statistically adjusted to make up for an undercount of roughly 5 million people, many of them minorities in dense urban areas who tend to vote for Democrats."

Conservatives worry that, having learned from the failure of Bill Clinton's high-profile push for census sampling, the administration has adopted a stealth approach.

The stakes are huge. Census figures determine each state's seats in Congress, the district boundaries for political office, plus how the states divvy up $300 billion in federal aid. Statistical sampling might shift up to 30 seats in the U.S. House of Representatives. That shifts votes in the Electoral College, too, affecting presidential outcomes as well.

Rep. Darrell Issa (R-Calif.), ranking member of the committee overseeing the census, called Groves's selection "incredibly troubling [because it] contradicts the administration's assurances that the census process would not be used to advance an ulterior political agenda."

Undercounts are hotly political. The Left argues that minorities and illegal immigrants are usually undercounted. They seek statistical "adjustments" to add made-up people, using assumptions and formulas that can be both factually wrong and politically manipulated. You might not get counted, yet your tax dollars could be spent to count millions of fictitious people.

The Supreme Court Has Not Answered the Sampling Question

Is statistical sampling constitutional?

The Supreme Court dodged the question in 1999. Its ruling enabled the then Republican Congress to block President Bill Clinton's sampling plan for the 2000 census. But the narrow ruling left room for a future Congress and president to change the result.

By 5-4, the Court declared that current statutes do not permit sampling to decide how many seats each state would have in Congress. Left unaddressed were the Census Bureau's ability to adjust numbers that determine seats for legislatures and local governments, the drawing of congressional district boundaries (performed at the state level), and allocation of federal money.

Most importantly, the Court avoided ruling on what Article 1, Section 2 of the Constitution requires: "[An] Enumeration shall be made within three Years after the first Meeting of the Congress of the United States, and within every subsequent Term of ten Years, in such Manner as they shall by Law direct."

Does the last phrase leave wiggle room for sampling if the law is changed? The justices didn't decide, although Justice Antonin Scalia tried. "To give Congress the power ... to select among various estimation techniques having credible (or even incredible) 'expert' support, is to give the party controlling Congress the power to distort representation in its own favor," he wrote. Only genuine enumeration, according to Scalia, guarantees the "minimal possibility of partisan manipulation."

Any future ruling will come from a Supreme Court that includes an Obama appointee—and starts with built-in agreement from Justices [John Paul] Stevens, [Ruth Bader] Ginsburg and [Stephen] Breyer that sampling is okay.

The Potential for Political Tampering

Regardless of what courts may say, some think the country is safe from sampling because they believe there's not enough time for President Obama and his team to implement it. Is there? Clinton's Census Bureau in June 2000 posted plans in the *Federal Register* claiming that in nine months they "could hire sufficient staff and acquire the necessary equipment to complete census 2000 and produce statistically corrected redistricting numbers by the April 1, 2001, statutory deadline." The Obama team currently has almost 23 months from now to meet the April 1, 2011, deadline.

Congressman Patrick McHenry (R-N.C.) believes the danger is real. As ranking member on the subcommittee that

Why People Support or Oppose Statistical Sampling

The debate over census methods, rightly or wrongly, has been recast as a partisan, racial, and regional battle. Historically, the headcount has produced a differential undercount—that is, an undercount of racial minorities and other groups, such as renters and children. Advocates of "sampling," in particular, view statistical adjustment as a way of rectifying bias in the headcount. Opponents view such statistical methods as avenues of manipulation and as creating more inaccuracies in the census than they remedy.

With respect to reapportionment and redistricting, how one answers the question "how to count" is often highly correlated with one's answer to the question "who stands to benefit." The state of Utah was against the use of imputation [a type of statistical sampling used in the census to insert missing data to determine population numbers], for example, only after it realized that redoing the census without imputation would allow it to have one more congressional seat. (Not a peep was heard while the [Census] Bureau was using imputation to construct the apportionment totals and the resulting winners and losers were unknown.) Similarly, large cities and states with large minority populations are often forceful advocates of statistical adjustment because they think their representation in either Congress or state legislatures will increase as a result or that a greater share of federal or state dollars will be directed their way.

Nathaniel Persily, "The Law of the Census: How to Count, What to Count, Whom to Count, and Where to Count Them," Cardozo Law Review, vol. 32, no. 3, January 2011.

oversees the census, McHenry describes a scenario whereby sampling is offered as an emergency remedy for problems after the census is taken next April.

The Government Accountability Office recently told Congress that problems "threaten the accuracy" of the census. Plans to use handheld computers have already been scaled down, requiring a reversion to pencil and paper.

The Democrats who chair the key House committee and subcommittee—Reps. Edolphus Towns (D-N.Y.) and William Clay (D-Mo.), say they are "deeply concerned that the Census Bureau will not be able to complete its constitutionally mandated responsibility." Their Senate counterpart, Sen. Tom Carper (D-Del.) calls it "an impending state of emergency."

Another worrisome sign: In March, the Census Bureau named ACORN [Association of Community Organizations for Reform Now], the liberal group accused of registering thousands of nonexistent people to vote in 2008, as one of its "national partners" to help count heads.

With its impact on dozens of congressional seats, the Electoral College, and the allocation of billions in taxpayer dollars, the possibility of sampling demands attention. The potential for political tampering and manipulation is too huge to ignore, whether those in power have pure intentions or Machiavellian intent.

As Joseph Stalin said, "Those who cast the votes decide nothing. Those who count the votes decide everything." And so could those who count the voters.

"At least some members [of Congress] have indicated that any such exclusion [of noncitizens from consideration for apportionment] would have to be done through constitutional amendment since the Constitution otherwise requires total population as the basis for apportionment."

Unauthorized Immigrants Must Be Included in the Census

Margaret Mikyung Lee and Erika K. Lunder

With the estimated population of unauthorized immigrants in the United States rising on an annual basis, much controversy surrounding the decennial census revolves around the question of whether these individuals should be counted and if their numbers should be used to apportion congressional seats. While opponents argue that counting illegal immigrants distorts the population counts and thus apportionment, Margaret Mikyung Lee and Erika K. Lunder contend in the following viewpoint that the

Constitution mandates that illegal immigrants must be counted, and their numbers should be considered when drawing districts and allotting congressional seats to states. Through careful analysis of the founders' language, which calls for the enumeration of "persons," the authors conclude that had they wanted to only count "citizens," the founders would have used this specific term, which appears elsewhere in the Constitution, when establishing the basis for the decennial census. In addition, Lee and Lunder find no existing precedent that would preclude unauthorized immigrants from the census count. Lee is a legislative attorney who has written extensively on immigration and immigrants' rights for the Congressional Research Service (CRS). Lunder is a legislative attorney who has also contributed to many reports for CRS.

As you read, consider the following questions:

1. As stated by the authors, as it is used in the Constitution, how is the term "citizens of the United States" related to the term "persons/people"?

2. How do "debates surrounding the original Apportionment Clause and the Fourteenth Amendment" give further credence to the broad interpretation of the term "persons," according to Lee and Lunder?

3. According to the authors' analysis, how does the *Wesberry v. Sanders* Supreme Court case ruling support the continued count of unauthorized immigrants for apportionment?

This memorandum provides a brief analysis of whether unauthorized aliens must be included in the decennial census required by article 1, section 2, clause 3 of the Constitution, as amended by the Fourteenth Amendment. The Constitution requires the census determine the "actual enumeration" of the "whole number of persons" in the United States, with the data used to apportion House seats and direct taxes among the states. The apportionment calculation is based on the states' total resident population, with individuals (both citizens and noncitizens) counted at their "usual residence."

"Persons" and "Citizens" Are Not Synonyms

It appears the term "persons" in the original Apportionment Clause and Fourteenth Amendment was intended to have a broad interpretation, and it is likely broad enough to include unauthorized aliens. It seems clear "persons" is not limited to "citizens" as the Framers would have likely used that term instead had it been their intent. The Constitution uses both the terms "persons/people" and "citizens of the United States," and the terms do not seem intended to be interpreted identically—"citizens of the United States" appears to be a subset of "persons/people." Courts have generally held that noncitizens, including unauthorized aliens, are "persons" in the context of other constitutional provisions, including other parts of the Fourteenth Amendment. While it does not appear that any court has decided the meaning of the term "persons" for apportionment purposes, a federal district court did state in dicta [remarks] that the term clearly includes unauthorized aliens.

It could be argued that unauthorized aliens should not be included in the category of "persons" for purposes of apportionment because of their legal or voting status. On the other hand, historically, those without the right to vote or with inferior legal status, including women, children, and convicts, have been included. Furthermore, the fact that slaves were to be partially counted when they enjoyed few rights seems to suggest the Apportionment Clause language was intended to be broadly inclusive. Similarly, the fact that the Framers felt compelled to specify the exclusion of "Indians not taxed" may suggest "persons" was understood to otherwise include individuals residing within a state, regardless of legal status. Thus, it can be argued [as in the case *Federation for American Immi-*

gration Reform v. Klutznick] that "[b]y making express provisions for Indians and slaves, the Framers demonstrated their awareness that without such provisions, the language chosen would be all-inclusive."

The debates surrounding the original Apportionment Clause and the Fourteenth Amendment add further support for the conclusion that the term "persons" was intended to be broadly interpreted. The Framers adopted without comment or debate the term "persons" in place of the phrase "free citizens and inhabitants" as the basis for the apportionment of the House, thus suggesting the term "persons" includes free citizens and any other individuals who would be considered "inhabitants." According to James Madison, apportionment was to be "founded on the aggregate number of [the states'] inhabitants." During the debate on the Fourteenth Amendment, Congress specifically considered whether the count was to be limited to persons, citizens, or voters. The term "persons" was used instead of "citizens" due, in part, to concern that states with large alien populations would oppose the amendment since it would decrease their representation. Another concern with using the term "citizen" was that it "would narrow the basis of taxation and cause considerable inequalities in this respect. . . ." Congress may also have been influenced by the fact that aliens could vote in some states. Congress has subsequently considered excluding noncitizens from the apportionment calculation on several occasions, and at least some members have indicated that any such exclusion would have to be done through constitutional amendment since the Constitution otherwise requires total population as the basis for apportionment.

There Is No Precedent for Excluding Noncitizens from the Census

The argument could be made that counting unauthorized aliens as "persons" for apportionment purposes dilutes the

Undocumented Immigrants Boycott the Census

The National Coalition of Latino Clergy and Christian Leaders, which represents 22,000 pastors in 34 states, is calling on millions of undocumented immigrants and sympathizers to boycott the 2010 census in protest of government inaction on passing comprehensive immigration reform. "We can assure you that over 3 million participants and members of our church will not participate," says Reverend Miguel Rivera, the coalition's head.

The census does not ask participants about their immigration status, and the bureau insists that all information is confidential and strictly protected by law. Rivera maintains, however, that participation puts the undocumented at risk.

"They are liars. They have been lying for years," Rivera says of census officials' assurances. "People in our churches are being hunted like animals," he says. "Undocumented immigrants should not take more chances."

Jill Colvin, "Down for the Count," First Things: A Monthly Journal of Religion & Public Life, no. 202, April 2010.

voting power of citizens in states without significant numbers of unauthorized aliens and, therefore, is inconsistent with the Supreme Court's decision in *Wesberry v. Sanders* that requires congressional districts be drawn equal in population to the extent practicable (i.e., "one person, one vote"). However, *Wesberry* and its progeny involve intrastate, as opposed to interstate, disparities, and the Court has indicated in another line of cases that the *Wesberry* standard does not apply to interstate apportionment. Because each state must have at least one

House district and a fixed number of representatives must be allocated among all states, votes in states with populations less than the ideal district are "more valuable than the national average" and it is "virtually impossible to have the same size district in any pair of States, let alone in all 50." Therefore, while the goal of "complete equality for each voter" under the *Wesberry* standard is "realistic and appropriate for state districting decisions," the Court has explained that it is "illusory for the Nation as a whole." While this second line of cases does not address the specific issue of whether illegal aliens must be counted for apportionment purposes, they seem to undermine the argument that *Wesberry* and its progeny require their exclusion.

Some have pointed to the fact that the census has historically included questions about citizenship, thus perhaps suggesting that a distinction has been made between citizens and noncitizens for purposes of counting individuals. It is true that at least two early censuses (1820 and 1830) included a category for foreigners not naturalized and later censuses asked about place of birth. However, such information was not used to exclude any noncitizens from the census count. Rather, it is clear that such individuals were included in the total count, and it appears the data was collected for informational purposes (similar to how information was collected about age, occupation, etc.). It does not appear that unauthorized aliens have been excluded from any census.

> *"Rather than apportioning congressional seats among the states on the basis of the full count of the decennial census, a more logical distribution would be on the basis of the number of native-born and naturalized U.S. citizens."*

Noncitizen Counts Must Not Be Used to Determine Congressional Apportionment

Jack Martin

In the face of the continually increasing unauthorized immigrant population in the United States as well as an influx of legal noncitizen residents, the government should reform the ways that it apportions congressional seats to states, argues Jack Martin in the following viewpoint. Martin notes that under the current system, the decennial census counts all individuals living in a state, whether legally or illegally, citizen or noncitizen, and allots congressional representatives to that state based on the total population. He contends that this number distorts apportionment because the illegal immigrants as well as the noncitizen residents do not have the right to vote and already have repre-

sentation from the governments in the countries from which they came. He adds that this method of distributing seats based on total number of individuals living in a state dilutes the voting power of citizens living in areas with low numbers of immigrants and should be stopped to preserve the integrity of the US government. Formerly a US diplomat, Martin now serves as director of special projects for the Federation for American Immigration Reform.

As you read, consider the following questions:

1. As stated by the author, how would the 2000 election results have been different if apportionment was based only on citizens living in the country?

2. By how many people and what corresponding percentage did the foreign-born population of the United States increase in 2006, according to Martin?

3. According to the author's calculations, which states would gain and which would lose congressional seats under the current census count methodology versus the citizen only count?

M ost Americans do not realize that illegal immigrants are also represented by members of the U.S. House of Representatives. How can that be? It is because by interpretation of statute the constituency of representatives is based not just on the number of citizens but also on noncitizen foreigners residing in the United States, including illegal alien residents. This practice results in granting illegal aliens and other noncitizens equal weight with citizens in their electoral representation.

Rather than apportioning congressional seats among the states on the basis of the full count of the decennial census, a more logical distribution would be on the basis of the number of native-born and naturalized U.S. citizens. If this were done, states with large numbers of illegal aliens and other noncitizens would lose seats to states that have a higher share of citizens.

The interests of illegal aliens are not only represented in Congress. Mexico and other countries aggressively assert the right to represent their nationals illegally residing in the United States. Through the petition of Mexico, the International Court of Justice has asserted a right to weigh in on the rights of illegal immigrants in the United States. A plethora of national and community-based organizations across the country regularly defend the presence of illegal aliens and work for laws to offer them various protections including amnesty. In addition, our legal system provides access to counsel for indigent illegal aliens in criminal proceedings.

All US Citizens Should Have Equal Representation

As a result of the current apportionment system, a representative from an area of the country with very few illegal aliens represents many more U.S. citizens than a representative from a metropolitan area with a large number of illegal aliens. Thereby, U.S. citizens in the low-illegal alien areas have a diminished share of representation than their counterparts in the high-illegal alien districts. For example, in the Dover metropolitan area, the residents in 2000 were 98 percent either U.S. citizens by birth or naturalization. In the San Diego metropolitan area, 87.3 percent of the residents were U.S. citizens. The share of citizens was even lower (84%) in El Paso County, Texas, in 2000. This is a form of unequal representation of U.S. citizens.

However, the law governing the composition of congressional districts does not say that all residents of the United States will be the basis for determining the size of congressional districts. Excluded from the representation system are, ". . . Indians not taxed." This exclusion is analogous to the exclusion from U.S. citizenship governed by the 14th Amendment that specifies that all persons, ". . . subject to the jurisdiction . . ." of the United States acquire our citizenship when born in the United States. That phrase, ". . . subject to the jurisdiction . . ." excluded Indians living in tribal nations among others.

Whether it was the intent of the framers of the Constitution or subsequent amendments to provide representation of illegal aliens in the U.S. House of Representatives would make an interesting legal discussion. Nevertheless, it is clear that changing the current system to remove the unequal representation of U.S. citizens in that body is a political issue that needs to be pursued in the political arena. Regardless of whether that change should be launched by amending the current statute governing apportionment or through a constitutional amendment, it should be pursued.

Counting Noncitizens Has Changed Election Results

FAIR's [Federation for American Immigration Reform's] analysis of the 2000 census data upon which the 2000 apportionment of congressional seats was based, found that:

> If the seats in the House of Representatives were reapportioned based on the distribution of U.S. citizens, the big loser of seats would be California, losing 6 seats. Three other states with large immigrant populations both legal and illegal would also lose one seat each, i.e., Texas, New York and Florida. The winners in this reallocation of congressional representation would be the residents of Indiana, Kentucky, Michigan, Mississippi, Ohio, Oklahoma, Pennsylvania, South Carolina and Wisconsin. Those states each would gain one additional representative.

Since the 2000 census, both legal and illegal immigrants as well as other nonimmigrant residents have continued to pour into the country. In 2000, one in every eleven residents in the

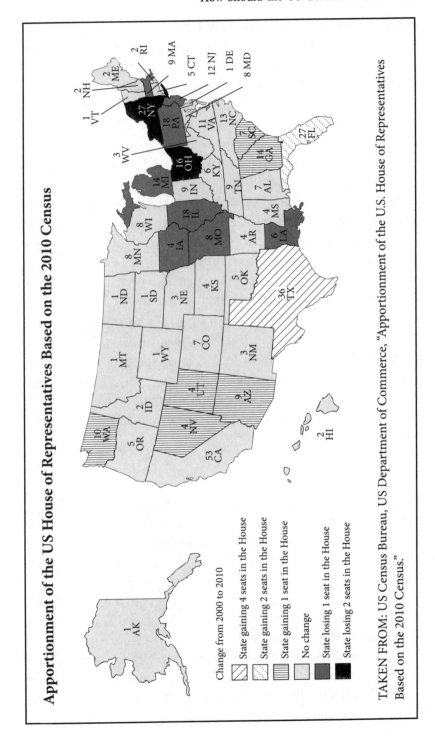

Apportionment of the US House of Representatives Based on the 2010 Census

Change from 2000 to 2010

State gaining 4 seats in the House

State gaining 2 seats in the House

State gaining 1 seat in the House

No change

State losing 1 seat in the House

State losing 2 seats in the House

TAKEN FROM: US Census Bureau, US Department of Commerce, "Apportionment of the U.S. House of Representatives Based on the 2010 Census."

country was foreign born. Today the share is one in every eight residents is foreign born. As a result, even though there has also been an increase in the number of immigrants gaining U.S. citizenship, representation of U.S. citizens in Congress will be even further distorted if the 2010 census is used for apportionment in the same way that the 2000 census was used.

In 2000, there were 31.1 million foreign-born residents in the country. Of these, 12.54 million (40.3% of the foreign born) were naturalized U.S. citizens. If the 18.57 million non-citizens were excluded from the apportionment, the above described results would have changed not only apportionment in Congress, but also the composition of the Electoral College that elects the president, because that is based in part on the composition of the House of Representatives.

In the 2004 presidential election, based on the 2000 census apportionment, the Electoral College awarded reelection to President [George W.] Bush by a vote of 286 to 251. If the apportionment had been made on the basis of U.S. citizens and the above described changes in apportionment had occurred, President Bush would have received an additional five Electoral College votes.

Coming Shifts in Apportionment

The influx of legal and illegal immigrants and other foreign nonresidents has continued and has increased since 2000. The Census Bureau estimates on the basis of the American Community Survey (ACS) that in 2006 the foreign-born population of the country had increased to 37.55 million residents—an increase of 20.7 percent. This contrasts with a 4.6 percent increase in the native-born population. The 2006 ACS data also shows that the naturalized foreign-born population had increased since the 2000 census by 25.7 percent. Nevertheless, despite the increase in naturalizations, the number of non-U.S. citizen residents also increased—by 3.2 million persons, 17.3 percent.

If the current system of equal proportion apportionment of congressional seats is maintained, the projected population in 2010 of about 313 million residents will result in the following states gaining seats:

- Arizona (2)

- Florida (2)

- Georgia

- Nevada

- Texas (4)

- Utah

The states that will lose those 11 seats are:

- Illinois

- Iowa

- Louisiana

- Massachusetts

- Michigan

- Missouri

- New York (2)

- Ohio (2)

- Pennsylvania

Note that the immigrant gateway states of California and New York do not stand to gain further seats from the immigrant influx—and New York in fact stands to lose representatives. This is because in this decade the flow of immigrants—both legal and illegal—has shifted to less immigrant-saturated states, and the wave of immigrants to these states has slowed.

However, if apportionment were done on the basis of equal proportion representation of U.S. citizens in 2010, the results would be very different. The states that would gain seats then would be:

- Indiana

- Iowa

- Louisiana

- Michigan

- Missouri

- Montana

- Ohio

- Oregon

- South Carolina

Those nine seats gained would be lost by the following states:

- Arizona

- California (4)

- Florida

- New Jersey

- Texas (2)

Note that the net swing is greatest in the states with major concentrations of illegal immigrants. Arizona instead of gaining two seats would lose one. California would lose four seats. Texas instead of gaining four seats would lose two—a net difference of six fewer seats. Florida instead of gaining two seats would lose one—a net reduction of three seats.

It should also be kept in mind that any change in the distribution of representation in the House of Representatives has an effect on the composition of the Electoral College. The question that flows from that observation is whether it is appropriate that illegal foreign residents should continue to be accorded weight in the selection of the U.S. president?. . .

It should be noted that the distortion of representation of U.S. citizens described above applies as well within each of the states. This distortion results from using the same decennial Census Bureau count of all residents in creating the districts of state legislative delegates and senators. States, however, are not governed by the same federal apportionment laws, although it must be noted that the U.S. Supreme Court has ruled that states may not permit unequal representation.

Just as some groups advocate that states should allow noncitizens to vote, others might argue that it is improper to give representation to noncitizens in drawing up the districts of state elected officials.

Only Apportionment Should Be Reformed

The distribution of political power in our federal system of government logically should rest on representation of U.S. citizens. Foreign nationals residing in our country, whether legally or illegally, are represented by their governments, many of which allow their citizens to vote and hold public office in their home country while residing in the United States.

Inertia and the lack of public awareness of the distortion to representation of U.S. citizens in the U.S. House of Representatives must be overcome if Congress is going to be motivated to take up this reform issue. It seems likely that a large majority of U.S. citizens would support such a change if they realized that the current system increasingly dilutes their representation in Congress with each additional arrival of an illegal alien or foreign guest worker.

The current system of apportioning congressional seats should be changed to reflect only the distribution of U.S. citizens. To do so would not require any change in the data col-

lected by the U.S. census, and such a change could leave unchanged the system of using census data on all residents to
allocate federal public assistance.

> "The particular results of the census are descriptive, but the categories that produce those results are prescriptive: They tell Americans how they are expected to think of themselves and of each other."

The Census Should Reform Its Racial Categorization of Americans

David A. Hollinger

In the following viewpoint, history professor David A. Hollinger argues that the categorization of race should be dropped from the US decennial census and renamed "population groups" or "primary identity groups." He believes that these broad groupings would begin to de-emphasize race as a categorization. As a second step to this reform, Hollinger calls for an end to "panethnic" groupings that ignore the distinctions between individuals from a single region with unique cultural identities and challenges based on their country of origin. By removing the categorization of race and renaming it in a more general but nuanced fashion, the author envisions movement toward a new conversa-

David A. Hollinger, "Race, Politics, and the Census," *Chronicle of Higher Education*, vol. 52, no. 28, March 17, 2006, pp. B6–B8. Copyright © 2006 by David A. Hollinger. All rights reserved. Reproduced by permission.

*tion about and understanding of the intricacies of American
identity. Hollinger is the chairman of the Department of History
at the University of California, Berkeley and author of the book*
Postethnic America: Beyond Multiculturalism.

As you read, consider the following questions:

1. According to the author, when was the last time the US
   government participated in a "major debate" about race?

2. What are some of the "considerations" identified by the
   author as weakening the "case for panethnic categories"?

3. What two "causes" were forced into conflict as a result
   of the mixed-race issue?

What distinctions among people in the United States really matter? The U.S. Census Bureau provides the official answer: Americans are white, black, Asian-American,
American Indian, or Hawaiian and Pacific Islander, unless
they are Hispanic, in which case they can also be any of the
above. The census forms include dozens of questions about
age, gender, household income, and a host of other aspects of
an individual's life, but the survey leads off by asking respondents to locate themselves in this "racial" system. The tabu-
lated results for that single question on race are by far the
most widely noted of the multitudinous findings of the census.

Does the census make the right distinctions? We need to
be sure because the categories it uses are a touchstone for
countless public and private institutions and programs. The
particular results of the census are descriptive, but the categories that produce those results are prescriptive: They tell
Americans how they are expected to think of themselves and
of each other.

Invigorated Debate on Race and the Census Is Needed

Our social scientists, historians, and political philosophers remind us constantly that the central significance of a census is not the statistics it yields, but the distinctions it draws within a national population. So it is important to get the categories right. They should match an understanding of our nation and its public policies that can be vindicated through open debate.

Yet the bulk of the public, encouraged by a remarkably uncritical news media, continues to believe that the federal census is descriptive, a body of objective facts about the nation. In an era when scholars have subjected race and ethnicity to unprecedented scrutiny, critical public assessment of the key decisions of the Census Bureau has been remarkably muted. Discussion has focused on only a few of the relevant questions, especially the status of people of mixed ancestry and whether Hispanics are a race or an ethnic group. The entire system of racial and ethnic classification employed in the federal census has not received the more deliberate and sustained public debate that it deserves. The option of checking more than one box, introduced in the 2000 census, begged entirely the question of how the boxes are labeled. The time is right: The 2010 survey will soon be upon us.

I want to argue for two basic reforms of the census categories. They may be controversial. But I believe even those who might not be persuaded by my proposals can accept my chief point: that we need a real debate about the census.

What are the issues too often ignored? How do I think the census should look in 2010, if revised in the light of recent scholarly discussions of race and ethnicity?

The US Government Ignores Race

My first specific proposal, offered by many others before me, concerns the very concept of race. What the news media and many Americans refer to as race is at the center of American life. But the Congress of the United States has not had a major debate about it since the civil rights era of the late 1960s and early 1970s. The Census Bureau, which is the federal agency most responsible for defining race, would rather not talk about it. Too many of the people who want to classify and count are unable to agree on why we need to do it, are unwilling to offer a forthright public justification for it, cannot even present a coherent and convincing defense of the specific categories they want to use, and fail to explain why the concept of race is still viable. No wonder the forces demanding an end to the counting of Americans by race, or by any descent-related category, are growing. A ballot initiative to that effect was narrowly defeated in California a few years ago, but the issue is far from dead there and in other states.

The government takes an ostensibly commonsense view of the matter, eschewing any and all connections to what science has to say, as in this statement of 1992, which remains in effect: "The concept of race as used by the Census Bureau reflects self-identification; it does not denote any clear-cut scientific definition of biological stock. The data for race represent self-classification by people according to the race with which they most closely identify. Furthermore, it is recognized that the categories of the race item include both racial and national origin or sociocultural groups."

The Scientific Definition of Race

But common sense has its limitations. The concept of race has had a tough time from scholars for some time now. The American Anthropological Association's executive board, for example, issued a "Statement on Race" in 1998, noting that conventional geographic racial groupings differ from one another in only about 6 percent of their genes. Science has long since established, in the words of the anthropology statement, that "present-day inequalities between so-called 'racial' groups are not consequences of their biological inheritance but products of historical and contemporary social, economic, educational, and political circumstances." Since the concept of race carries so much pseudo-biological baggage, it is often said that we are all better off without it.

To be sure, the concept is often defended as a social construct. Yet social constructivists can go in several directions. If we abandon race, don't we risk pretending that the inequalities created by the process of racialization are less severe than our social science and our history show them to be? Other social constructivists, suspicious of narratives of victimization that assign group-defining power to oppressors, place more emphasis on a given group's own agency as a "race." Different social constructivists thus want to retain the term for opposite reasons, one to mark the power of racists to racialize and demean people of a given descent, and the other to mark the substantiality of a community and the integrity of its efforts to survive as a solidarity.

More portentous for the viability of the idea of race are recent voices in the biomedical sciences. The concept still has genuine utility, we are told, once it is separated from the mistakes and prejudices of old-fashioned racial science. What the biomedical defenders of race have in mind is quite different, however, from the meaning of the term implied by all varieties of social constructivists. "To biologists," explains the University of Chicago professor Jerry A. Coyne, in an issue of the *Times Literary Supplement* last year, "races are sets of populations within a species that are both geographically separated and differ genetically in at least one trait"—such as "skin and eye color, and color and form of the hair." Those thoroughly physical distinctions sometimes matter in diagnosing disease. "Sickle-cell anemia," Coyne observes, "is most common in blacks whose ancestors came from Equatorial Africa"; it is a mutation, he says, a mutation that "resulted from natural selection in response to malaria in tropical Africa."

The more credibility in our time is achieved by a distinctly biological usage of race, the less credible the arguments for the word's other uses. The invidious history of race, and the likelihood that it will continue to have some currency in science—when it is separated from what is now seen as the false biology once associated with it—undercuts the hopes of social constructivists for the idea's progressive uses.

Redescribing Race

Hence we have a remarkable situation: There is a prevailing, popular assumption that we can continue to use the word "race" because everybody knows what it really means, while in truth nobody has valid grounds for assuming a common understanding of its meaning. One might suppose that those honest uncertainties would lead the Census Bureau to drop the word "race" altogether. I believe it should.

This reform would not be so hard to enact, even while preserving every other aspect of the existing system. Respondents could be asked to mark one or more of the six basic categories (non-Hispanic white, black, Asian-American, American Indian, Hawaiian and Pacific Islander, and Hispanic), but those categories could be described simply as "population groups" or "primary identity groups." They might even be described as "racial and ethnic groups." That last phrasing would be the weakest version of the reform because it retains race, but even it would at least erase the race-ethnicity distinction and eliminate the need for the anomalous treatment of Hispanics as an ethnic group that could be of "any race." It would also diminish the pressure to have Latinos classified as a race, because in this scheme they would be in no danger of losing equal standing in the census with the groups currently called races. Surely such a reform would solve more problems than it would create. . . .

The Problems with Panethnic Categorization

The concept of race is not the only point at issue. Another is the justification for classifying and counting people by large, "panethnic" categories like Asian-American and Hispanic rather than simply by smaller, more sharply defined descent groups like Chinese-Americans and Mexican-Americans. It is abundantly clear that current classifications are political artifacts masquerading as natural kinds. "Hawaiian and Pacific Islander" was added to the list (and classified as a race) for the 2000 census when Sen. Daniel K. Akaka, a Democrat from Hawaii, insisted upon it and presented evidence focusing on the discrimination suffered by persons in that category.

It is imperative to remember that the number of these panethnic or racial groups can be expanded by sheer force of political lobbying. Kenneth Prewitt, a former director of the Census Bureau, points out in an issue of *Daedalus* last year that Hawaiians and Pacific Islanders are not the only group that can make a credible case for a distinctive history and a record of being abused. Since the whole enterprise of ethnic and racial classification has long since turned its back on science, Prewitt observes, "it is difficult to arrive at a public consensus on how many racial and ethnic groups there are in America." Are Jews a race? If not, why?

Other considerations weaken the case for panethnic categories. The borders among the standardized groups have become less vivid as a result of increases in marriage and reproduction across group lines. No wonder the internal diversity of all such groups is increasingly visible to researchers and journalists. But new immigration, too, is relevant here. The practice of lumping all Asian-Americans together and all Hispanics together was put in place before the huge post-1970 immigration brought large numbers of distinctive descent communities into the United States from Asia and Latin America. Today we have Chinese-Americans, Korean-

Americans, and many other Asian-derived groups. The same case can be made about Hispanics: Americans include people who trace their ancestry to Mexico, Cuba, Venezuela, and other specific places of origin.

In the context of such realities, one might press several related questions. How should we classify Americans who trace their descent to Pakistan or Iraq or Turkish Anatolia? If they are not Asian-Americans, are they in the white category? Do we need a Middle Eastern panethnic category? How might the Arab population be classified? What is the status of people whose ancestry is Brazil, or Portugal, or Spain? Are they all Hispanics?

The Question of Race
Should Be More Specific

There is a way around those dilemmas. It involves a second reform of the census, more radical than the first, which deals only with the concept of race. The census might drop some or all of the six large panethnic categories that now define what everyone calls "the race question," and count instead those inhabitants who identify with descent communities from specific countries or regions, such as China or Mexico. This reform need not overturn the "check more than one" option; respondents could still do that, but on the basis of different categories. Any public or private agency that wished for any reason—including the design and enforcement of antidiscrimination remedies—could combine the number of people who selected Cuba, Guatemala, Mexico, Puerto Rico, etc., and have a functionally Hispanic set of statistics. Yet such an agency would have the capacity to deselect from a certain program Portuguese-Americans and Spanish-Americans, for example, if it chose to do so, on the ground that they are of European background and thus less eligible for ethno-racial benefits. The same would apply to Americans who selected China, Egypt, India, Iran, Japan, Korea, Morocco, Pakistan, the

Latinos' Dilemma with the Census Question of Race and Ethnicity

U.S. Latinos exhibit a diverse set of national origins, cultural affiliations, racial self-identifications, and linguistic varieties. Cultural self-identification most often derives from one or more of the following categories: Native American/indigenous, Anglo-European, or Black, though the range extends to an assortment of cultures, subcategories, and alternative self-designations. The environment in which one lives also impacts racial awareness. Latinos are born into or migrate into neighborhoods and social environments in which they are perceived through a national and regional racial lens.

But the census only tracks ethnic and racial self-identification via a set of standard categories. Self-identification of ethnicity and race is a datum reliant on folk conceptions, on personal levels of scientific literacy, and on a complex set of cultural and psychological, sociocultural, economic, and political factors. The categories used by the census to provide data regarding "race" raise significant dilemmas for the large number of Latinos who do not see themselves as fitting within these categories and for all who discount any reference to a term that they find unscientific, anachronistic, muddled, and/or distressing to invoke.

Ramón Solórzano Jr. and Sondra Ahlén,
"Latino Questions on Race, Ethnicity,
and Language at the Advent of the 2010 Census,"
Harvard Journal of Hispanic Policy, vol. 22, 2009–2010.

Philippines, Syria, Vietnam, etc. Aggregation is possible, depending on the mission of the agency using the census data and the salience to that mission of the distinctions among East Asians, South Asians, and Middle Eastern Asians.

What about persons of African descent? There is no compelling reason not to simply list "Africa" as among the choices, since most Americans of African descent do not identify with specific countries or regions within sub-Saharan Africa, and since statistics about persons of African descent are by far the most pertinent to antidiscrimination remedies. Black Americans, and they alone, are the heirs of a multi-century history of group-specific enslavement and hyperracialization (seen in the invidious classification on the basis of "one drop of blood") carried out under constitutional authority in the United States. Other census questions dealing with immigration can provide at least some data distinguishing recent immigrants from Africa and the Caribbean and their descendants from African-Americans with a heritage affected by slavery and Jim Crow [laws]. "Europe" would do well enough for what has been called white, although a listing of descent from particular European national identities and those heavily derived from Europe, such as New Zealand and Australian identities, is also a reasonable way to measure the uniquely privileged white population of the United States, and subject to aggregation depending on one's purpose. American Indians, already a category of exceedingly porous boundaries, could remain unchanged or listed by specific tribe.

Such a more particularized system would recognize the identity claims of a great number of specific communities of descent within the populations to which the panethnic terms like Asian-American and Hispanic are blind. It might enable authorities to measure more accurately the progress of specific descent groups in overcoming the obstacles of white racism and economic hardship, and thus help target remedy to wrong. More information of such a refined sort, now available only in fragments through the less prominently displayed and less frequently answered "national origin" segment of the census forms, would better enable public and private agencies to determine where disadvantage lies and what causes it.

Our social scientists regularly explain how different are the destinies of various immigrant populations in the United States for example, from Korea as opposed to Cambodia, or from the poor rural counties of Mexico as opposed to Cuba. The goal of equality might be better served if agencies could use stronger census data to decide how to focus their energies, rather than being obliged to work with data organized into categories the very selection of which was made on the basis of a prior judgment about what groups were disadvantaged. In our current system, the Census Bureau has the de facto role of deciding in advance which Americans are eligible for entitlements. A key to the special status given to Hawaiians and Pacific Islanders, after all, was the evidence of their victimization.

More Nuance Is Necessary

In developing the case for these two reforms, I have been speaking about the census categories as if their major justification was to advance the cause of equality in general, and to facilitate antidiscrimination remedies in particular. I have also mentioned the role of those categories in registering the cultural identity of individual Americans. Yet both of those purposes have been prominent only in the last half century, and neither purpose has ever been explicitly declared by the Census Bureau, nor by the congressional authorities to which the Census Bureau reports. Indeed the government of the United States persistently refuses to explain to the individuals filling out the census forms just why the information is being solicited.

In the context of such uncertainty, the mixed-race lobby grew and finally persuaded the Census Bureau to allow for the "check more than one" option. Mixture was virtually irrelevant to enforcing antidiscrimination remedies because in the eyes of many potential discriminators, a recognizable trace of ancestry was enough. But the public was allowed to suppose that a major purpose of the census was, instead, to register personal feelings of identity. Who can say that was mistaken? The government provided little reason for people to think they were wrong.

As a result, mixed-descent activists had to struggle against civil rights organizations that might otherwise have been their natural allies. The cause of equality and the cause of identity were allowed to come into conflict with one another. The Census Bureau did not provide respondents with a way to deal with each issue separately, did not clarify the role of the census in relation to either, and did not even explain that the two issues got in each other's way if both were addressed through answers to a single census question.

Would the specific reforms I suggest here be fully responsive to the demographic complexities of the American society? Of course not. It is easy to identify complexities these reforms ignore and confusions they might create. But those complexities and confusions need to be critically assessed in comparison with those of rival systems, especially the system now in place. In 2000 the political scientist Peter Skerry argued in his book *Counting on the Census?* that the census is "an inherently political undertaking" that should be made the subject of open, political debate informed by the most reliable knowledge available. No such thing happened then. Will it now?

| "This open question finally erases the 18th-century racial hierarchy, dispenses with the slippery term race itself, easily allows self-expression and can happily embrace multiple identities."

The Census Question on Race Should Be Open-Ended

Kenneth Prewitt

One of the most controversial questions on the decennial census asks respondents to report their race or ethnicity. Many critics, such as Kenneth Prewitt, argue that this multiple-choice approach to race restricts individuals' ability to express the race or ethnicity with which they identify and stifles the national conversation on race. In the following viewpoint, Prewitt extends this argument, suggesting that the current system of five racial categorizations and one ethnicity confines understanding in the country to outdated definitions of race. He proposes an open-ended question that allows each individual to identify with the races or ethnicities that are most meaningful to him or her. He believes this method of questioning will provide a more accurate picture of racial and ethnic identification in the country and advance debate on this issue. Prewitt was the director of the US

Census Bureau during the 2000 census and is currently a professor of public affairs at Columbia University.

As you read, consider the following questions:

1. How has America's classification of race on the census evolved since the country's founding, according to the author?

2. What does Prewitt identify as some of the practical uses of statistics on race gained through the census?

3. What are some of the distinctions Prewitt believes could be made by making the race question on the census open-ended?

The successful 2010 census left millions of Americans puzzling over its face question. Many disliked declaring any race; others were uncertain which box fit them; some wondered why the government even asked their race. In fact, the question does not work well, and we can do better. But first, how did we get here?

Eighteenth-century science ordained a hierarchical ordering of five human "races." At America's founding, given legal and demographic realities, it counted three in its first census in 1790: White, Black, Red. It added a fourth race in the mid-19th century when, driven by hysteria over the "yellow peril," the distinct Chinese and Japanese nationalities blurred into the catchall Asian race, which then became the census home for additional Asian nationalities.

Mid-20th-century civil rights policies that statistically measured racial discrimination needed to accommodate people from the Caribbean and Mexico, so the strange Hispanic/Non-Hispanic ethnicity-but-not-a-race question was shoehorned into the mix. Multiculturalism in the 1980s put pressure on census categories, especially on behalf of a multiracial choice, leading the 2000 census to introduce the mark-one-or-more option.

Out of this history came our current classification, which uses color (White and Black); civil status (Native American enrolled tribe); nationality (Chinese, Japanese, Filipino and six more) summarized as two umbrella races—Asian and Pacific Islanders; and Hispanic ethnicity (with three nationalities listed).

The Complexity of the Race Question

But, asks the public: "*Why* does the government insist on sorting and counting us by race?" There is no simple answer because assorted purposes—each reasonable on its own terms—have been yoked to an archaic classification. These purposes trace to our history and to contemporary conditions. The tragedies of black slavery and Indian genocide left inequalities that racial justice policies are still trying to erase. Policy responses to disparities in employment, education, health and incarceration call for statistics on groups being left behind. Diversity goals in universities and businesses use census categories. How new Americans are assimilating is a further question answered with census statistics.

Beyond specific policy uses of census data, citizens see in the census an opportunity to express pride in their heritage. President Obama emphasized his African heritage by checking only one census box, rather than recognizing his dual black and white parentage. Social justice, social disparities, social assimilation and social pride are *all* folded into a census question based on the five 18th-century "races" of Black, Brown, Red, Yellow, White and a question insisting that there are only two ethnicities in America: Hispanic/Non-Hispanic. No wonder the questions puzzle and irritate.

Some demand that the questions be dropped altogether, expecting this to magically produce a color-blind society. But when discrimination penalizes groups because of their color, ancestry or immigrant status, a nation committed to fairness will not choose to be statistically ignorant of these facts.

Let People Define Race on Their Own

The next census, however, doesn't have to repeat today's questions. It should simply ask:

What national origin, ethnicity, tribe, language group or ancestry do you consider yourself to be? (List all those important to you.)

This open question finally erases the 18th-century racial hierarchy, dispenses with the slippery term race itself, easily allows self-expression and can happily embrace multiple identities. This question doesn't assume that a recently arrived Ethiopian belongs to the same race as 10th generation descendants of enslaved people from Africa's Gold Coast. It doesn't put fifth generation Chinese Americans into the same race box as first generation Vietnamese. It doesn't count an Argentinean who speaks only English the same way it treats a Mayan immigrant. From the open-ended responses, answers can be categorized in the various ways that make sense depending on public purposes at hand, even reconstructing the five 18th-century races if that is desired.

This open-ended question should be paired with questions on immigration status:

Where were you born, and where were your parents born?

This question, combined with the one above, tells us how immigrant status interacts with national origin, ethnicity or language group, so that we can eliminate barriers as 21st-century newcomers follow the path marked out by Italians and Irish a century ago, or Germans and Swedes a century earlier.

Unfortunately, neither Congress nor the Obama White House will initiate a serious national conversation about today's patched together racial classification. "Too political," they will conclude. But America's universities, think tanks, advocacy organizations and news media can supply the intellectual work we need to ensure that carefully designed questions will provide information relevant to the public purposes that justify asking the questions in the first place. And if one day everyone simply writes "American," the color-blind society will have arrived by public choice.

A statistical portrait of how different groups are faring remains necessary both to erase the inequities of historical racism and to prevent discrimination as the recently arrived strive to participate fully in their new country—but only if we draw the portrait more carefully than that produced by the 2010 census.

Periodical Bibliography

The following articles have been selected to supplement the diverse views presented in this chapter.

Michael Barone	"Count on the Constitution," *Washington Times*, February 24, 2009.
Carl Bialik	"Making It Count: Alternative Ways to Gather Census Data," *Wall Street Journal*, July 31, 2010.
Gilda Daniels	"Census 2020: How Would You Reform the Census? Perspectives: Expand the Racial Categories for Classification," *Insights on Law & Society*, Winter 2010.
Haya El Nasser	"Senators Try to Exclude Illegal Immigrants from 2010 Census," *USA Today*, October 14, 2009.
Nathan Glazer	"Do We Need the Census Race Question?," *Public Interest*, Fall 2002.
Sam Kean	"Can the Census Go Digital?," *Science*, October 15, 2010.
Eliza Krigman	"Census Games," *National Journal*, April 11, 2009.
Bill McGurn	"Our Racially Divisive Census," *Wall Street Journal*, June 8, 2010.

For Further Discussion

Chapter 1

1. Terri Ann Lowenthal and John W. Whitehead take opposing views on the significance of questions on the US census. Whitehead argues that the census no longer simply counts heads for the purposes of representation; it now gathers personal information that the government seemingly does not need or have a right to obtain. Lowenthal, on the other hand, insists that census questions pertaining to race, income, disability, and other personal topics help the government allocate funding to civic projects that cater to community needs based on such responses. Find out what questions the Census Bureau asks on its decennial census and the American Community Survey (both forms are available online) and explain whether you believe the inquiries are intrusive and unnecessary or appropriate and helpful.

2. After rereading the first four viewpoints in this chapter, explain whether you think the conduct of the current census has remained within the boundaries set forth by the Constitution. In your analysis, explain whether you believe the census should be permitted to gather information not specified in the Constitution. Citing arguments from the viewpoints, substantiate your claim.

3. Morley Winograd maintains that the US census has become a pawn of partisan politics. He insists the controversies over the census focus mainly on the struggle between keeping personal information private and divulging enough information to provide the government with enough data to target aid where it is needed. The *Economist* points out that when national censuses throughout

history have gathered information from citizens, the intentions have not always been altruistic. Do you think releasing too much information to the US government could result in tragedies similar to what the *Economist* evokes? What kinds of problems, if any, do you foresee? Thoroughly explain what leads you to your conclusions.

Chapter 2

1. After reading through the viewpoints in this chapter, which group do you think is most underserved by census data? Referring to evidence in the viewpoints, what reasons can you give to explain why this group lacks representation? Explain what you think are the negative consequences of this undercount. Finally, explain how you would rectify the problem.

2. Racial classification questions on the US census have been a controversial issue for decades. In the viewpoint by Haya El Nasser, several commentators express their gratitude that respondents to the 2010 census were allowed to mark more than one racial category when identifying themselves. Susan Saulny, however, worries that allowing expanded racial categorizations on the census may lead to statistical errors when this data is compared to other surveys that have more narrow classifications. Explain how you feel about broadening racial classifications on the census. What reasons can you provide to justify your position? You may quote freely from the viewpoints.

Chapter 3

1. In the first two viewpoints in this chapter, the authors debate whether statistical sampling, a technique in which a small subset of the population is used to make generalizations about the larger population, should be used when conducting the decennial US census. Jordan Ellenberg focuses his defense of statistical sampling on showing that it

is a tested and reliable scientific method. Ernest Istook concentrates mainly on the fact that sampling will not count each individual one by one. After reading the two viewpoints, whose argument do you find more convincing? From what you have read, do you think that statistical sampling has a proven track record that makes it an appropriate tool to use in the enumeration of the population, or must every person be counted individually? Do you think sampling could produce more accurate results? Why or why not?

2. In the decennial census count, unauthorized immigrants as well as citizens from other countries living legally in the United States are all counted. Margaret Mikyung Lee and Erika K. Lunder provide an argument as to why this count is constitutional. However, Jack Martin contends that considering these noncitizens when determining congressional representation skews the apportionment of representatives. Reread the viewpoints and formulate your own opinion on this issue. Do you agree that the individuals in question must be counted as part of the census? If you believe they should be counted, what should their numbers be used to determine? Are there any other problems or benefits you can think of that arise from counting these individuals alongside American citizens?

3. One of the questions on the census form that spurs the most heated debate is the question regarding race. After reading the fifth and sixth viewpoints, what do you think should be done to resolve this issue, or does anything even need to change at all? Do you agree with Kenneth Prewitt who argues that the census question should be open-ended or do you side with David A. Hollinger who contends that the question on race should be dropped altogether or at least be reworded? Do you foresee any problems with either of these solutions? Support your answer with quotes from the viewpoints.

Organizations to Contact

The editors have compiled the following list of organizations concerned with the issues debated in this book. The descriptions are derived from materials provided by the organizations. All have publications or information available for interested readers. The list was compiled on the date of publication of the present volume; the information provided here may change. Be aware that many organizations take several weeks or longer to respond to inquiries, so allow as much time as possible.

American Statistical Association (ASA)
732 North Washington Street, Alexandria, VA   22314-1943
(703) 684-1221 • fax: (703) 684-2037
e-mail: asainfo@amstat.org
website: www.amstat.org

The American Statistical Association (ASA) is an international organization of statisticians who work together to further develop, apply, and disseminate information about statistical science. While their work ranges far beyond the US census, the organization has advocated for US government initiatives that would make the US Census Bureau an independent agency no longer under the umbrella of the Department of Commerce. ASA contends that this would allow for greater accountability and functionality of the bureau. Information about this stance can be found on the organization's website.

Brookings Institution
1775 Massachusetts Avenue NW, Washington, DC   20036
(202) 797-6000
website: www.brookings.edu

The Brookings Institution is a nonprofit, public policy think tank that carries out research with the goal of strengthening the American democracy; improving welfare, security, and opportunities for Americans; and encouraging an international system that allows for open cooperation while maintaining prosperity and security. The organization's coverage of the 2010 census focused on providing unbiased information about the importance of the national count of the population and reporting the census results. Articles such as "Census 2010: Counting for Dollars," "Five Myths About the 2010 Census and the U.S. Population," and "A Pivotal Decade for America's White and Minority Populations" can be read on the Brookings website.

The Census Project

Communications Consortium Media Center (CCMC)
401 Ninth Street NW, Suite 450
Washington, DC   20004-2142
(202) 326-8700 • fax: (202) 682-2154
e-mail: info@ccmc.org
www.thecensusproject.org

Run by the Communications Consortium Media Center, the Census Project has sought to provide up-to-date information about the buildup to, execution of, and follow-up to the 2010 census. The stakeholders of the project believe the census to be a valuable tool to collect information about the US population and have tried to inform policy makers on the national and state levels of its value. The Census Project website provides fact sheets and a blog, as well as news briefs concerning the 2010 census.

Census Scope

www.censusscope.org

Census Scope is a project of the Social Science Data Analysis Network, an association of universities that seeks to make census data accessible to educators, policy makers, and the public through a range of media. The Census Scope website allows visitors to search maps, charts, and rankings to explore the most recent and past census findings. Detailed information about population growth, income, language, and race among other topics can be found on the website.

Federation for American Immigration Reform (FAIR)

25 Massachusetts Avenue NW, Suite 330
Washington, DC   20001
(202) 328-7004 • fax: (202) 387-3447
website: www.fairus.org

The Federation for American Immigration Reform (FAIR) is an organization made up of members who believe that US immigration policy reform—particularly strengthened border security, ending illegal immigration, and limiting overall immigration levels—is necessary for the nation to thrive. With regard to the census, the organization argues that illegal immigrants as well as foreign nationals should not be counted because recognizing these noncitizen members of the population distorts congressional apportionment. Reports on this issue can be read on the FAIR website.

Funders' Committee for Civic Participation (FCCP)

221 NW Second Avenue, Suite 207, Portland, OR   97209
(503) 505-5703 • fax: Attention FCCP (503) 505-5648
website: www.funderscommittee.org

The Funders' Committee for Civic Participation (FCCP) is an organization working to increase civic participation nationwide, particularly in typically underrepresented communities, to ensure the strength and continuity of the American democracy. While the emphasis is mainly on voting and electoral systems, with the 2010 census, the FCCP focused also on encouraging these same groups to participate in the count to ensure that their communities received needed government funding and representation. The FCCP website provides extensive information about the census and participation rates in the categories of updates, resources, in the news, census results, and featured reports. This project also created the Census Hard to Count 2010 website, which provides interactive maps of the United States illustrating where these populations live and their rates of participation.

Leadership Conference on Civil and Human Rights

1629 K Street NW, 10th Floor, Washington, DC   20006
(202) 466-3311
website: www.civilrights.org

The Leadership Conference on Civil and Human Rights is an association of more than two hundred national organizations seeking to ensure that the civil and human rights of all US citizens are observed and protected. Through its legislative advocacy, the coalition works to enact progressive change nationwide. Leading up to, during, and after Census 2010, the conference worked to ensure that historically undercounted groups, including minorities and low-income people, were represented in the national enumeration of the population. General information about the significance of the census and its results, resources to help achieve an accurate count, and tools for education can be found on the organization's website.

Population Reference Bureau (PRB)

1875 Connecticut Avenue NW, Suite 520
Washington, DC   20009
(800) 877-9881 • fax: (202) 328-3937
e-mail: popref@prb.org
website: www.prb.org

The Population Reference Bureau (PRB) works to provide current demographic information about populations around the world so that those populations can use that data to ensure their own well-being and that of future generations. In accordance with this goal, the PRB covers the US decennial census by publishing results from the survey, reports on the progress of preparations for the census prior to its execution, and suggestions for future improvements to the enumeration process. Reports such as "2010 U.S. Census Data Machine Springs into Action," "The U.S. Decennial Census and the American Community Survey: Looking Back and Looking Ahead," and "First Results from the 2010 Census" can be read online.

Prison Policy Initiative
PO Box 127, Northampton, MA 01061
website: www.prisonpolicy.org

Prison Policy Initiative is a nonprofit organization dedicated to informing the public about the dire consequences of mass incarceration on the United States. Specifically, the organization has focused on providing details about how the census's counting of prisoners where they are jailed instead of in their hometowns has distorted the decennial enumeration of the population. Prisoners of the Census, one of the organization's projects, focuses on this issue and how it impacts the drawing of congressional districts and the apportionment of representatives. Findings and reports are published on the organization's website.

US Census Bureau
4600 Silver Hill Drive, Washington, DC 20233
(301) 763-4636
website: www.census.gov

Created in 1902, the US Census Bureau is the US government agency charged with carrying out the decennial census as well as more frequent surveys of the population. The data the bureau collects is used to apportion federal congressional seats to the states, determine necessary community services, and distribute funds to these localities. Details about the various surveys conducted by the agency can be found on the Census Bureau website along with the findings of these surveys.

Bibliography of Books

Margo J. Anderson
The American Census: A Social History. New Haven, CT: Yale University Press, 1988.

Margo J. Anderson and Stephen E. Fienberg
Who Counts? The Politics of Census-Taking in Contemporary America. New York: Russell Sage Foundation, 2001.

Kenneth Darga
Sampling and the Census: A Case Against the Proposed Adjustments for Undercount. Washington, DC: AEI Press, 1999.

D. Sunshine Hillygus, Norman H. Nie, Kenneth Prewitt, and Heili Pals
The Hard Count: The Political and Social Challenges of Census Mobilization. New York: Russell Sage Foundation, 2006.

Sarah E. Igo
The Averaged American: Surveys, Citizens, and the Making of a Mass Public. Cambridge, MA: Harvard University Press, 2007.

Herbert S. Klein
A Population History of the United States. New York: Cambridge University Press, 2004.

Les Krantz and Chris Smith
The Unofficial U.S. Census: Things the Official U.S. Census Doesn't Tell You About America. New York: Skyhorse, 2011.

Jeff Manza and Christopher Uggen

Locked Out: Felon Disenfranchisement and American Democracy. New York: Oxford University Press, 2006.

Melissa Nobles

Shades of Citizenship: Race and the Census in Modern Politics. Stanford, CA: Stanford University Press, 2000.

Joel Perlmann and Mary C. Waters, eds.

The New Race Question: How the Census Counts Multiracial Individuals. New York: Russell Sage Foundation, 2002.

S. Karthick Ramakrishnan

Democracy in Immigrant America: Changing Demographics and Political Participation. Stanford, CA: Stanford University Press, 2005.

Clara E. Rodriguez

Changing Race: Latinos, the Census, and the History of Ethnicity. New York: New York University Press, 2000.

Cheryl Russell

Demographics of the U.S.: Trends and Projections. 3rd ed. Ithaca, NY: New Strategist Publications, 2007.

David A. Swanson and Paula J. Walashek

CEMAF as a Census Method: A Proposal for a Re-Designed Census and an Independent U.S. Census Bureau. New York: Springer, 2011.

Kim M. Williams

Mark One or More: Civil Rights in Multiracial America. Ann Arbor: University of Michigan Press, 2006.

Index